the KINGDOM of HEAVEN

an Analysis of the Message of the New Testament

V. KERRY INMAN

Arbuta House
1040 Arbuta Rd., Abington, PA 19001

Quotations from the following are used by permission:
The *Holy Bible, New International Version.* Copyright © 1978 by New York International Bible Society.

ISBN 0-913551-00-7

Copyright © 1983 by V. Kerry Inman

Printed in the United States of America

Published by
Arbuta House
1040 Arbuta Road
Abington, Pennsylvania 19001

to

Irene

*my love and my help
whose encouragement has made
this book possible*

Table of Contents

List of Study Aids 7
Preface 9
Chapter 1   Salvation and Revelation 11
Chapter 2   The New Testament Period 19
Chapter 3   John and Jesus 31
Chapter 4   The Present Kingdom 39
Chapter 5   The Growing Kingdom 47
Chapter 6   The Coming Judgment 57
Chapter 7   The Preaching of the Apostles 63
Chapter 8   Paul and the Message of Jesus 71
Chapter 9   Paul and Judaism 77
Chapter 10 The Necessity of Christ 85
Chapter 11 The Shadow and the Reality 95
Chapter 12 The Covenant and the Dispensation 103
Chapter 13 The Long Wait 115
Bibliography 123

Study Aids

The Land of Israel in the Time of Christ (Map)	13
From Malachi to the Apostles (Time Line)	21
The Mustard Seed and Plant (Illustration)	49
An Exercise In Understanding How The New Testament Uses the Old	70
The Rebellion of 66 A. D. (Map)	87
The Roman Empire in the 1st Century A. D. (Map)	117

Preface

The Kingdom of Heaven is the premier publication of Arbuta House. It would not have been possible without the help of many people who assisted in making it a reality.

I would like to say thanks particularly to the following: Dr. Richard B. Gaffin, Jr. who first introduced me to biblical theology. My colleagues Drs. Perry G. Phillips and James J. McCloskey who read the entire manuscript and made helpful criticisms. (Any weaknesses in this book are probably due to my failure to listen to the above named individuals.) Mr. Clyde W. Snyder for the cover design. Miss Shari L. Reiss for the maps and charts. Mrs. Doris Calverley, Miss Gail Foor, and Miss Phyllis Leithead for typing the manuscript. And, Harmony Press, Inc. of Phillipsburg, New Jersey for the printing.

V. Kerry Inman
Arbuta House, 1983

Intro: Survey, yes. But not of contents...
Message! [Go to Discussion ? # 4 — ask...]

1

SALVATION AND REVELATION

Biblical Texts: John 14:1–14; 5:31–47; Luke 24:36–49

In John 14:1–14 Jesus asserts that he has a special relationship with God the Father. Knowing him is knowing God. He is the way to the Father.

In John 5:31–47 Jesus speaks of those who testify concerning him. He says that John the Baptist testified about him, more important than that, the work which Jesus himself does testifies about him. Finally, he says the Scriptures testify about him— even Moses wrote about him.

Luke 24:36–49 is the account of Jesus appearing to his disciples after the resurrection and explaining to them how all the Law of Moses, the Prophets, and the Psalms spoke about him and how it was fulfilled in his work.

I.

When Jesus spoke to his disciples and said, "I am the way and the truth and the life (John 14:6 NIV)," it was very clear what the central point of Jesus' message was—the central point of Jesus' message *was Jesus*. Jesus' teaching did not center around a body of ideas, religious tradition, or particular rites. Jesus' message was that he, among mankind, had a special relationship with God. But it was more than just a special relationship. Jesus said, "I am in the Father and the Father is in me." To understand this is to understand the message of the New Testament.

We must recognize the centrality of Christ before trying to understand what the New Testament says and what it means for us today.

All that the New Testament says is either about Christ or based on what he did and taught.

In recognizing the centrality of Christ to the New Testament message, we also recognize the central theme of the Scriptures as a whole. As Christ indicated in John 5:45 Moses spoke of him, and as is taught in Luke 24:44, the prophets and writers of psalms also spoke of him. <u>Christ taught that he was the central theme of the Bible. In him are united the New Testament and Old Testament.</u>

But recognizing the centrality of Christ is only the very first step in beginning a study of the New Testament. <u>An important second step is deciding upon the method to be used</u>. There are many ways that we could approach a study of the New Testament.

Types of New Testament Study

Some studies of the New Testament, or of the Bible, focus on <u>background information</u> such as the description of the life and times of Jesus. Others may consider each book of the New Testament as to its <u>author, date, and the like.</u> More often when one wants to understand the *message* of the New Testament, one is inclined to take an approach to study which could be described as "systematic."

<u>Systematic studies</u> of the Bible are those which attempt to determine what the Bible says on a particular subject such as God, salvation or the last days. They examine verses in the Bible on the subject and try to come to conclusions about the over all teachings of the Scriptures.

A second method of studying the *message* of the New Testament is called <u>"biblical-theological."</u> The quite awesome sounding name might make it seem like this is the exclusive ground of theologians and seminary students, but actually the biblical-theological approach is quite simple. <u>This approach attempts to study the message of the New Testament as it was progressively revealed.</u> This is to say that one would first study what John the Baptist said and did, then what Jesus said and did, and then what the apostles said and did. A biblical-theological study is one that <u>sees the revelation of God as it unfolds.</u>

12

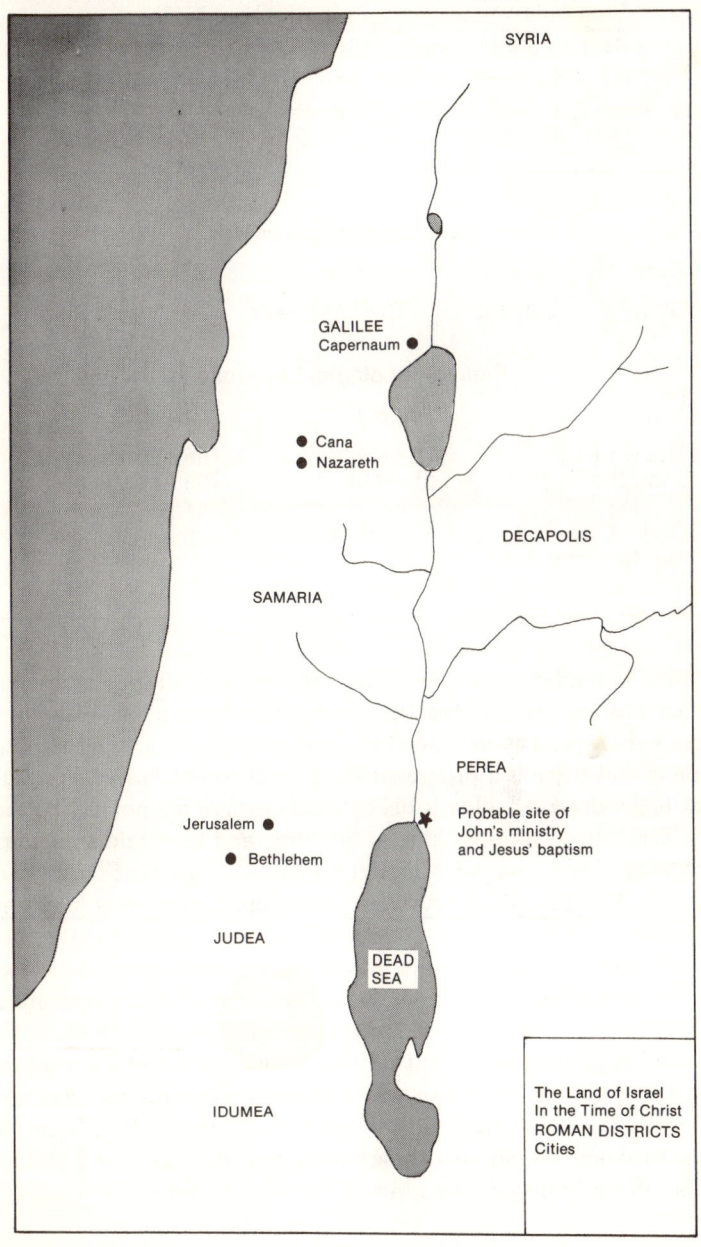

There is an assumption in this method, and that is that the Scriptures did not fall from heaven as a finished book. They were written by men over a period of years. The whole picture was not presented at first, but as time went on men received more and more of the message which God was revealing to them.

Systematic Approach

Topic 1	Topic 2	Topic 3	Topic 4
God	Salvation	The Last Days	The Holy Spirit

Biblical-theological Approach

Topic 1	Topic 2	Topic 3
The work of John the Baptist	The Ministry of Jesus	The Ministry of The Apostles

God, Salvation, Christ, etc. studied as themes developing throughout

---

In this textbook we are following the biblical-theological approach to the study of the New Testament message. As was stated above there is an assumption involved in this method. The assumption is that there is a progressive character to revelation. We must not misunderstand what is being said here. We are not saying that the Scriptures said one thing at one time and then said something contradictory to that later on. But rather *we regard the Scriptures as a unity.* What is said at one time is developed more fully later on.

We may perhaps illustrate this in the teachings of Jesus. In two places in the New Testament, Jesus says that Moses wrote about him. The first is in John 5:45, and the second is in Luke 24:44. In the first passage Jesus makes this statement, but it is not said that he explains it. In the second passage we find that some of his disciples were upset by the events that had transpired with the death of Jesus. He then explains to them that these events were necessary and fulfilled what Moses had said about him.

What these two accounts show is, that Jesus taught (in the first case) that Moses wrote about him—but this was not fully developed. If it had been, then the disciples would have understood the events surrounding the death and resurrection. In the second case, Jesus does not teach something different—he develops what was taught earlier. Later on in the book of Acts, we see some of Jesus' disciples teaching about Christ from the books of Moses.

The biblical-theological approach to the study of the Bible tries to trace the development of teachings. Topics are considered as themes running through the history of revelation.

In this discussion we have already made some indications of stages in the unfolding of revelation. We need now to get a better look at these stages. John the Baptist has already been mentioned as a step, but there is actually an earlier one. The whole Old Testament is important to understanding the message of the New Testament. John, Jesus, and for the most part the apostles, all preached to people who were educated in the Old Testament. The immediate impact and meaning of their message can only be fully appreciated when we understand what was on the minds of the people of that day. The first step in the unfolding of revelation is the Old Testament.

A second step, as has been noted, is the ministry of John the Baptist. His work was preparatory to Christ's, and we want to see how his work helped to prepare people for the message that Christ was to bring later.

Jesus' own message is of tremendous significance. As Christians we are fully aware of the significance of Christ's saving work, but often we are quite ignorant of what Christ taught. We are interested in studying Christ's work, but we also want to understand what Christ said about his work.

With the ascension Christ's earthly ministry ended, and the burden of proclaiming it to the world became that of his apostles. But within the time of the apostles, we see progress in the unfolding of revelation: the Church grew and began to include Gentiles in great numbers, the old temple at Jerusalem was destroyed marking a great

15

c. change in the center of Judaism, and persecution made it evident that the <u>fullness of the kingdom</u> which Jesus proclaimed would not come without a long and difficult struggle.

The Unfolding of Revelation Today

(canon) The process of God's revealing his plan for eternity and will for mankind has been <u>complete</u> for centuries. Yet there is a sense in which it is "still going on" today. When people become Christians, their understanding of the Bible is usually very simple. It probably only consists of knowing that the Bible is about God and Jesus, contains the Ten Commandments, the Golden Rule, and the Twenty-third Psalm. At the time it is sufficient for one to know that in the Bible God teaches that all have sinned, that we must confess those sins and look to God for salvation through the work of Jesus Christ. Then the process of growing in grace begins. God does not want us to stay in this infancy. Paul speaks of <u>milk and the meat</u> of the gospel. The new-born babies need the milk, but those who are maturing need the meat.

In this book we will deal with revelation as it unfolds. It will not be a book of milk only, but it will attempt to provide an overview of the Scriptures which will introduce meat into the diet of the growing and provide more meat to the grown.

Questions for Review

1. What is the central theme of the New Testament? *Jesus* Of the Bible? *Jesus* Of the message of Jesus? *Jesus*

2. What are the basic assumptions of the biblical-theological approach to the study of the Bible? *1- progressive character of revelation 2- stages in unfolding*

3. What are three passages of Scripture which show Christ as the central theme of the Bible? *Jn. 14, Jn. 5, Lk. 24*

4. Compare and contrast the biblical-theological method of Bible study with any other method. *Background info.; Introductory ?'s; systematic*

5. What are some stages in the unfolding of New Testament revelation? *1- Whole O.T. 2- John the Baptist 3- Jesus 4- Apostles*

Questions for Discussion

1. This book is using a biblical-theological approach to Bible study rather than a systematic approach. What do you think would be the advantage of a systematic approach? *Gather all rev. on one topic*

2. How do you think Jesus explained the Law of Moses as speaking about himself? The Prophets? The Psalms? *1- Ceremonial types 2- Answer to Israel's fall 3- Xt as Mediator*

3. Do you feel that there are more assumptions involved in the biblical-theological method than are discussed in this chapter? *One Cov. of grace No moralism*

Intro. 4. When this study is completed, it will be helpful to look back at what one's previous ideas about the message of the New Testament were. Formulate what you now think is the basic message of the New Testament.

Concl. 5. What are your expectations for this course—that is, what do you hope to be able to do that you cannot now do?

2

THE NEW TESTAMENT PERIOD

Biblical Text: II Samuel 7

In II Samuel 7 we read God's response to David when he told the prophet Nathan that he wanted to build a temple for God. The response through the prophet was that David would not build the temple, but his son would build the temple. Some of the Jews in the time of Jesus were still looking for this son.

One problem that is encountered in trying to understand the Bible is that the events and circumstances belong to a distant time and culture. The culture was very different from ours, the people had different values, different goals in life, and at times it seems that they thought quite differently than we do today.

Many books have been written trying to describe the life and times of Jesus. It is important to understand the life and times of Jesus, but not just to get a picture of what the times were like. It is important for us to understand the thinking of the people of those times. We must understand their hopes and fears and the content of their faith. If we understand this, we will better understand the message of the New Testament.

Cultural Elements in Israel in the 1st Century A. D.

The culture of Israel in the time of Christ could be described as cosmopolitan—as being world wide in scope. Jerusalem as the religious center of Judaism, drew people from all over the Mediterranean and Near Eastern areas. The descendants of those Jews who had been dispersed in the centuries following the conquests by the Assyrians and Babylonians had settled in diverse lands. They often returned to Jerusalem on pilgrimages. In Acts chapter two, we read about Jews from various lands peoples who were present in Jerusalem on the day of Pentecost. Many cultural elements from these diverse lands came to influence the character of Judaism.

The cultural influences on Judaism may be grouped into four groups. These are:

1. Roman,
2. Greek,
3. Persian, and
4. Native Semitic.

Roman

The Roman influence on Judaism was the least significant. The Romans were basically military rulers. Their influence is seen in the New Testament when their military leaders and governors are mentioned. Roman philosophy and science were almost inseparable from that of the Greeks, and Roman literature had little apparent influence upon Judaism. The Romans as the ruling power, however, were responsible for the political situation under which Judaism found itself in the time of Christ, and this political situation had a definite effect upon Jewish thinking. Rome was seen as an enemy which eventually had to be thrown off if the promise of a Davidic king were to become a reality.

Greek

The Persian Empire, which Cyrus had established in the time of Daniel, was eventually conquered by the Greeks under Alexander the Great. The Greeks brought the Greek language and Greek thought to the whole Eastern Mediterranean area where it became the language of scholars and merchants. This language was rich in literature, philosophy, and science. Alexander built a city in Egypt

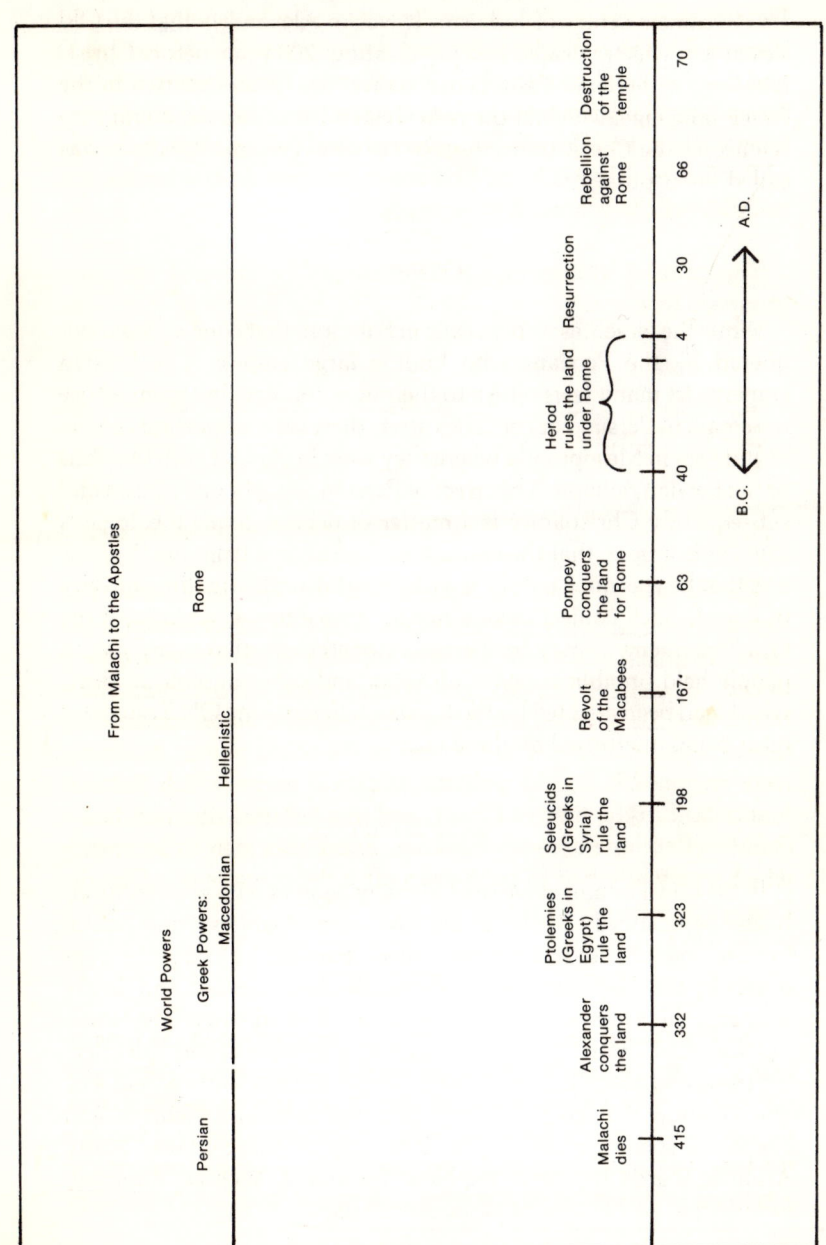

named after himself. This became the center of Greek learning. It also became a center of Judaism. It was in Alexandria that the Old Testament was translated into Greek about 200 years before Christ. Later when the New Testament was written, it was written in the Greek language. Much of the New Testament shows the literary influence of the Greek translation of the Old Testament, which was called the Septuagint.

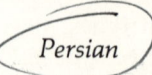
Persian

While the Israelites were in exile in Babylon, that country was conquered by the Persians who built a large empire. The Persian emperor let many Jews return to their own country, but many chose to remain in Persia. For centuries after, there were important centers of Judaism in Mesoptomia where they were in contact with the ideas of the Persian religion. The effect of Persian thought on Judaism and subsequently Christianity is a matter of debate. Some theologians say, for example, that the concept of Satan came from the Persians and that he was not a part of Jewish thinking until after the captivity in Persia. Such conjectures do not do justice to the integrity of the Old Testament. It may be the case, nonetheless, that many Jewish people held unbiblical views of Satan and other unbiblical ideas, which had been affected by the Persian religion—the Old Testament itself being unaffected by these ideas.

[Cyrus]

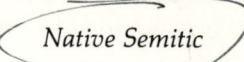
Native Semitic

In the Old Testament we read of many peoples who were culturally and linguistically similar to the Jews—the Moabites, Ammonites, Syrians, etc. These groups are called "Semitic." During the conquests by the Assyrians, Babylonians, Persians, Greeks, and finally Romans, these ethnic groups began to lose their identity. The Israelites scattered among them also began to lose some of their identifying traits and absorbed some things from their Semitic brothers. For one we know that the Jews lost their native language, Hebrew, and began to speak Aramaic, the language of the Syrians. Many Aramaic words appear in the New Testament, such as, *Rabboni, Ephphatha,* and *Eloi, Eloi, lama sabachthani.*

22

The Jews absorbed more than just the language of Syrians. They also absorbed the entire nation of Edom. Herod was an Edomite. They absorbed much that we do not know about, and many aspects of their thinking had probably been influenced by the ways of the nations about them.

What is significant in reviewing all of these cultural influences is that we recognize that Israel had changed a lot since the days of Moses. The New Testament times were culturally different from those of the Old Testament. Recognizing this helps us understand the New Testament, but it does not explain the origin of the New Testament. With all the influences upon Israel, it is important to realize that the Bible came from God. The Bible itself is the product of revelation—not cultural influence.

Judaism in the Time of Christ

In trying to imagine what the religion of people in the land of Israel was like just before the time of Jesus, we are apt to make several mistakes. One is that we sometimes think that before Jesus came, people believed that the Old Testament teaches exactly the same things we today believe it teaches. This is simply not the case. We must remember that we arrived at our understanding of the Old Testament through a conviction that Jesus was the Messiah, and we must remember that Jesus and his disciples contributed to our understanding of how Jesus fulfilled the Old Testament. Without this work of Jesus, people could not have understood the Old Testament in exactly the same way we do now.

Another mistake that might be made is to imagine that Jews, just before the time of Christ, believed what Jews do today. This is simply not the case either. Even though there are many things in the Jewish culture which go back much further than Jesus' time, the Judaism of that day was in many ways distinctly different from the Judaism of today.

The major distinction of the Judaism of Christ's day was *diversity*. The religion of the Jews in the time of Christ was not characterized by the relative unity of thought and practice which is found in

Judaism today. We have discussed several cultural influences on Judaism in the time just prior to Christ's appearance. These influences produced various forms of Jewish thought and practices which were quite diverse and often at odds with one another.

The various schools of thought in Christ's time did not all survive. One strain became the prevalent form and the others died out, but we have in the literature from that age some indications of the diversity which did exist. There are four strains which we can distinguish, but at the time there were probably more. These four are:

1) Rabbinic Judaism
2) Helenistic Judaism
3) Apocalyptic Judaism
4) Essene Judaism

Rabbinic Judaism

The strain of Judaism which contributed most to present day Judaism—indeed, is the very backbone of it—is Rabbinic Judaism. This represents the form of Judaism which was least influenced by non-Jewish thought and ethnic groups. In the time between the return from exile and Christ, there developed a serious and pious concern for keeping and living according to the law—the *torah* of God. Schools of teachers and students grew up in which the law was diligently studied. Particular attention was given to the problems of applying it in situations where the Scriptures had not spelled out in great detail what was to be done. A great body of oral laws, amplifying the Scriptures, arose.

These oral laws represent a sincere, honest attempt to be holy. It is unfortunate that we sometimes fail to appreciate this when we read of the Pharisees in the New Testament. Jesus came into conflict with these people who represented the strain of Rabbinic Judaism. He criticized them on two accounts—misuse of the oral law (Mark 7:9–13) and on a fundamental error in their concept of purity (Mark 7:18–23). But he also recognized their sincerity and devotion when he used them as the epitome of righteousness saying, "For I tell you unless your righteousness surpasses that of the Pharisees and the teachers of the law, you will certainly not enter the kingdom of heaven (Matthew 5:20 NIV)."

The proceedings of the great Rabbinic Schools became collected in the work known as the *Talmud*. This is the heart of modern Judaism. We can gain insight into this strain of Judaism from accounts in the Talmud. What follows is an account in the Talmud of an incident in a Rabbinic School at about the time of Christ. The students were discussing the requirement that Jews recite the prayer known as the *Shema* every evening. Imagine, if you will, the apostle Paul—who studied under Rabban Gamaliel—could have been one of the students mentioned here:

> A bridegroom does not have to recite the *Shema* on the first night or until the Sabbath is over, if he has not consummated the marriage. Once Rabban Gamaliel recited the *Shema* on the first night of marriage. His disciples said to him, "Master, didn't you teach us that a bridegroom is exempt from reciting the *Shema* on the first night?" He replied, "I will not listen to you, and cast off from myself the yoke of the kingdom of heaven for one moment."
>
> Berakoth 2:5, author's translation

For Rabban Gamaliel, keeping the law was part of the yoke of the kingdom of heaven. It was not something he followed only as required.

Hellenistic Judaism

When Alexander the Great conquered the Near East, he spread Greek ideas, Greek philosophy, and the Greek language to the land of Israel. As was mentioned before, Alexandria in Egypt became an important center of Greek learning and also of Judaism. It was inevitable that in Alexandria Greek influence on Jewish thought would become apparent. The following is a quote from a Jewish contemporary of Jesus, who lived in Alexandria, which shows Greek influence.

> Regarding Moses' account of creation, we must note several

matters. God understood beforehand that a good imitation could not exist without a good model. So when he determined to create the visible world, he first created a world which is only perceptible to the intellect.

On the Creation of the World, IV, Philo, author's paraphrase

The necessity of a pre-existing ideal "model" before the creation of something physical is purely Greek and foreign to native Semitic thinking.

Apocalyptic Judaism

A type of literature which developed in the period between the two testaments is apocalyptic literature. This actually has its origins in the Old Testament prophets such as Daniel and Ezekiel. Writers of apocalyptic literature displayed the hopes of Israel in a mystical fashion. Here is an example:

> The seven days passed; and the next night I had a dream. In my dream, a wind came up out of the sea and set the waves in turmoil. And this wind brought a human figure rising from the depths, and as I watched, this man came flying with the clouds of heaven . . .
>
> Next I saw an innumerable host of men gathering from the four winds of heaven to wage war on the man who had risen from the sea . . .
>
> After that, I saw the man coming down from the mountain and calling to himself a different company, a peaceful one. He was joined by great numbers of men, some with joy on their faces others with sorrow . . .
>
> This is what the vision means: The man you saw rising from the depths of the sea is he whom the Most High has held in readiness through many ages; he will himself deliver the world he has made, and determine the lot of those who survive . . . The day is near when the Most High will begin to bring deliverance to those on earth.

2 Esdras 13, extracts, New English Bible

Essene Judaism

One sect of Jews was known as the Essenes. Their exact character is uncertain, but many believe that they had much in common with the group of Jews who lived in the monastery at Qumran. These Jews regarded the rest of Judaism as apostate, and were looking forward to the coming messianic age. They thought that this was coming soon. They understood the Old Testament as teaching about this age. The following is an excerpt from one of the scrolls found in the caves at Qumran. It shows how they understood II Samuel 7:14.

> "I will be his father, and he will be my son." The "he" spoken of here is that descendant of David who shall work in Zion in the last days along with the Teacher of the Law. This is as the Scripture says, "In that day I will restore David's fallen tent (Amos 9:11)." These words refer to him who will arise to bring salvation to Israel.
>
> 3QFlor, author's paraphrase

Common Elements in 1st Century Judaism

Having shown different strains that were present in Judaism and emphasizing that there was diversity in Judaism, we must now recognize that the Jewish people, nevertheless, all had much in common.

The Importance of Revelation

All Jews recognized that God revealed things to men. The Rabbis saw this in their steadfast concern for the law. They knew the law, not because they believed they had superior judgment or intellect, but because they had the *torah*—God's law revealed to Moses at Sinai. The Hellenistic Jews, while dealing much with philosophical concepts, still recognized the fundamental difference between themselves and the Greeks. The Jews had God's law. It is difficult to understand the motivation of the writers of apocalyptic literature, but they understood that God spoke to prophets in dreams and visions (Numbers 12:6) even if their dreams and visions were not part of

God's revelation. And the Essenes, interpreting Scripture as they did, show us that they believed God revealed the truth about the future in the Scriptures.

The Messiah

All Israel was looking for the Messiah. Their expectations were not all the same. Some expected the Messiah to be a prophet, others a teacher of righteousness, others a kingly Messiah. Many of the things we see that the New Testament teaches about the Messiah were not present in the Jewish expectations. But the expectation of a coming Messiah was a unifying element in Judaism.

The Kingdom

Along with the messianic expectation is the expectation of the coming of the kingdom of heaven. The root of this expectation was in the prophecies of the Old Testament such as those in II Samuel 7. The Qumran sect saw in this a coming son of David—a coming king. Rabban Gamaliel mentions the kingdom of heaven not as something that will be ushered in by a king but as the reason for his prayers.

As we shall see in the next chapter, it is this kingdom expectation which shaped the first proclamation of the gospel. Both John the Baptist and Jesus begin their ministries with the words, "The kingdom of heaven is at hand."

Questions for Review

1. What were the major cultural influences on Judaism during the time of Christ? *Roman, Greek, Persian, native Semitic*

2. What are four strains of Judaism in the time of Christ? How are they alike? How are they different? *Rabbinic, Hellenistic, Apocalyptic, Essene*

3. Why is the knowledge of cultural elements important to a biblical-theological study? *Thinking, hopes, fears, faith/contents.*

4. What were the common elements of Judaism during the time of Christ? *Revelation, Messiah, Kingdom*

Questions for Discussion

1. How do you think the message of the New Testament might have been presented by John the Baptist if he came to a different cultural setting—such as ours? *Materialism, hedonism, narcissism*

2. Compare and contrast Judaism in the time of Christ with what you know of Judaism today. *Messianic expectation; unity; persecution*

3. Look again at the quotation on page 26 from 2 Esdras 13. This is part of the apocrypha. Of what use is this literature to the Christian? *Corroborative*

4. Has the information in this chapter changed your view of what the moods and attitudes of the times of Christ were like?

3

JOHN AND JESUS

Biblical Texts: Matthew 3:1-12; 4:12-17; 11:1-15; Mark 1:14-15

Matthew 3:1-12 is Matthew's account of the early part of John the Baptist's ministry.

Matthew 4:12-17 is Matthew's account of the beginning of Christ's ministry.

In Matthew 11:1-15 there is a description of an event in Jesus' ministry in which he comments on the work of John the Baptist. Mark 1:14-15 is Mark's account of the beginning of Christ's ministry.

John's Message

In the previous chapter we saw how the Jews had various beliefs and expectations. They expected a coming age, a kingdom of heaven. Each of the gospels begins with an account of John the Baptist, and John the Baptist is said to begin his message with the proclamation, "the kingdom of God is at hand." In the light of what we have learned in the previous chapter, this proclamation must have had tremendous impact! In the account of John's ministry we see that his preaching emphasizes three points: 1) The kingdom is at hand, 2) Repent and be baptized, and 3) One is coming.

The Kingdom is at Hand

In the gospels we run across the words "kingdom of God" and "kingdom of heaven" many times. In Matthew the phrase "kingdom of heaven" is used more often than "kingdom of God." At one time a group of theologians thought that there were <u>two distinct kingdoms</u> ? —the kingdom of God and the kingdom of heaven. It is quite evident on further study, however, that these phrases refer to the same kingdom. First, we know that at the time of John the Baptist the Jews <u>did not pronounce the name of God</u> found in the Old Testament (Hebrew: *Yahweh*) but rather used the word "Lord (Hebrew: *Adonai*). In chapter 2 we saw that in the *Talmud* a Rabbi speaks of the kingdom of heaven. This is apparently a way to avoid saying God's name. It is what is called a circumlocution. Secondly, with Greek speaking people there was no hesitation to use the word "God (Greek: *Theos*)" or to speak of the kingdom of God. From these facts we see that "kingdom of God" and "kingdom of heaven" are referring to the same kingdom—<u>one in a Greek way and one in a Hebrew way.</u> This is further evident in the accounts in two different gospels of the same event, one describing the proclamation of the kingdom of heaven, the other the kingdom of God (Matthew 4:17 and Mark 1:14). Matthew seems to use the words "kingdom of heaven" because, as many commentators have noted, he appears to have Jewish readers in mind.

<u>The important aspect</u>, however, of <u>John's proclamation is that this kingdom is at hand</u>. It is near. Some scholars have attempted to show exactly how near by studying the Greek word in the text. This is fine if one knows Greek, but apart from this we can determine that John the Baptist meant it was <u>very near—within the life time of the people then living—from two facts</u>. First, we see that the Jewish people <u>were expecting a kingdom.</u> John did not mean that some distant day a kingdom was coming—everyone knew this. Secondly, <u>John called the people to immediate action</u>—repentance and baptism. This immediate response would imply that the kingdom was coming immediately.

John's message, regarding the kingdom, was that it was coming very soon. The people of Israel were looking expectantly for a future day. Is it any wonder, then, that they turned out in great numbers to hear the man who said, "Repent, for the kingdom is at hand."

Repent and be Baptized

The second demand of John the Baptist's message was to repent and be baptized. We might at first think that this is a radical, new message as compared to the Old Testament. Where does the Old Testament teach repentance, or as Mark 1:4 says, "a baptism of repentance for the forgiveness of sins." Does not the Old Testament teach that sacrifices are the way to find forgiveness for sin?

To begin with it is only a common misunderstanding that the Old Testament sacrifices were viewed as the way to find forgiveness for sins. The prophets were clear about this.

> With what shall I come before the LORD and bow down before the exalted God?
> Shall I come before him with burnt offerings, with calves a year old?
> Will the LORD be pleased with thousands of rams, with ten thousand rivers of oil?
> Shall I offer my firstborn for my transgression, the fruit of my body for the sin of my soul?
> He has showed you, O man, what is good. And what does the LORD require of you?
> To act justly and to love mercy and to walk humbly with your God.
>
> Micah 6:6–8 NIV

The Old Testament people were required to offer sacrifice to God because of their sins, but the forgiveness of sins was to be found in repentance.

> Return, O Israel, to the LORD your GOD.
>   Your sins have been your downfall!
> Take words with you and return to the LORD.
> Say to him: "Forgive all our sins and receive us graciously,
>   that we may offer the fruit of our lips.
> "I will heal their waywardness and love them freely,
>   for my anger has turned away from them.
> I will be like the dew to Israel; he will blossom like a lily
>
> Hosea 14:1–2, 4–5a NIV

<u>Baptism too was not something entirely new</u> in the message of John the Baptist. Washing with water was a practice of the Israelites to make things ritually clean. Washing with water does make things physically clean, but in some instances it is clear that it is a ritual act symbolizing <u>making things acceptable for worship.</u>

> The Pharisees and all the Jews do not eat unless they give their hands a ceremonial washing, holding to the tradition of the elders. When they come from the marketplace they do not eat unless they wash. And they observe many other traditions, such as the washing of cups, pitchers and kettles, and dining couches.
>
> <u>Mark 7:3-4</u> NIV, footnote

John's baptism not the same as Jesus' baptism. Continuity, yes, but not identity

One is Coming

John's message was not self-serving. He pointed to the fact that <u>one greater than he was coming.</u> In the Gospel of John we read the account of John the Baptist being questioned as to who he was. When asked if he was the Messiah, he replied, "No." Then he was asked why he baptized, and he replied, "I baptize with water, but among you stands one you do not know. He is the one who comes after me, <u>the thongs of whose sandals I am not worthy to untie.</u>" (<u>John 1:26</u> NIV.) John's message pointed not towards himself but another.

In Matthew's account, John the Baptist says, "I baptize you with water for repentance. But after me will come one who is more powerful than I, whose sandals I am not fit to carry. <u>He will baptize you with the Holy Spirit and with fire.</u> <u>His winnowing fork is in his hand</u> and he will clear his threshing floor, gathering the wheat into his barn and burning up the chaff with unquenchable fire." (<u>Matthew 3:11-12</u> NIV.) In this statement we see that John saw that <u>the one who was coming was far greater than he.</u> His baptism was with water, but the coming one's would be with the Holy Spirit and fire. The following verse makes it clear that this means that he is coming

v.13 with blessing and punishment. He is coming to gather the wheat and burn the chaff.

Further on in the Gospel of John, John the Baptist says of Jesus,

34

"Look, the Lamb of God, who takes away the sin of the world! This is the one I meant when I said, 'A man who comes after me has surpassed me because he was before me.' I myself did not know him, but the reason I came baptizing with water was that he might be revealed to Israel." (John 1:29-31 NIV.) John's ministry in the final analysis pointed to Jesus as the Messiah, the Christ.

Jesus' Message

As was pointed out in the first chapter, the message of Jesus was about Jesus. He said, "I am the way and the truth and the life (John 14:6 NIV)." Jesus' message was properly about himself as he is the central focus of the whole Bible, but there are two things here that we should consider. First, not only is Christ's message important but his work—his acts—are important. Secondly, we understand Christ's significance not only from his message but from the whole of Scripture. Because of these two facts, we must understand that when we consider Christ's message we are only looking at that portion of his message which Christ himself made plain. The message of Christ is not the whole gospel, but it is the gospel as it was presented to the disciples by Christ. It was the gospel as it was presented to the first people who realized that Jesus was the Messiah. We must remember that there are many other things, that God revealed through the Scriptures, which teach about Christ.

[1. 2. Same was true of the O.T. - 'historical books']

As was stated in the first chapter of this book, we will be seeking to understand the message of the New Testament as it was progressively revealed. We have seen in chapter two what the state of the Jewish religion was just before the time of John the Baptist. In this chapter we have seen the message of John the Baptist. Next we must see Jesus' message and how it developed.

There are three elements we may point to as summing up Jesus' message. They are:

1) *The kingdom has come*, but in some ways
2) *The kingdom is still coming* and most importantly
3) *I am the way.*

We considered the third element in chapter one. In the remainder of this chapter and in the next, we will consider the first element. The second element will be considered in chapters five and six.

The Messages of John and Jesus

The Major Points of John the Baptist:

1. The kingdom of God is at hand
2. Repent and be baptized
3. One is coming

The Major Points of Jesus:

1. The kingdom has come
2. The kingdom is still coming.
3. I am the way

Remember that we are beginning our biblical-theological approach. Jesus' message included "repent and be baptized" in the early stages. What we are emphasizing, however, is the progression of revelation and have listed only the new elements of Jesus' message.

The Kingdom Has Come

Soon after his baptism by John the Baptist, Jesus began his ministry. The accounts of the earliest part of his ministry describe him as preaching the same message as John the Baptist. "Repent, for the kingdom of heaven is near (Matthew 4:17 NIV)." But it soon becomes evident that Jesus is more than just a disciple of John.

In Matthew 11;1–15, John sends his disciples to ask Jesus if he is the one who was to come or if they should look for another. The first impression one gets from this is that John is impatient. Jesus' response invokes the words of the prophets of the Old Testament regarding what would happen in the messianic era:

> Then will the eyes of the blind be opened and the ears of the deaf unstopped.
> Then will the lame leap like a deer, and the tongue of the dumb shout for joy.
> Water will gush forth in the wilderness and streams in the the desert.
>
> Isaiah 35:5–6 NIV

What is most significant in this passage is that after John's disciples had departed, Jesus speaks about the kingdom of heaven and says, "From the days of John the Baptist until now, the kingdom of heaven has been forcefully advancing, and forceful men lay hold of it (Matthew 11:12 NIV)." The point that is important here is that, not only is the kingdom near, but forcefully approaching.

Some time after this incident, another incident occurred in which Jesus teaches us concerning the kingdom of heaven. This is the incident recorded in Matthew 12:22-28. While casting out demons, Jesus is accused of doing such in the name of Beelzebub. Jesus responds with "But if I drive out demons by the Spirit of God, then the kingdom of God has come upon you (Matthew 12:28 NIV)." The obvious conclusions which the Pharisees should have made was that since Jesus cast out demons through the power of God, then the kingdom had in fact come.

This present character of the kingdom of heaven is a central point of Christ's message. One which relates to us today—we live in the Kingdom Age. Sometimes we become so caught up in the hope for the return of Christ, that we fail to see how significant his earthly ministry was—it ushered in a new age. We live in the age to which all the Old Testament people and prophets looked forward.

Questions for Review

1. What are the main elements of John's message? *[handwritten: 1. Kingdom is at hand. 2. Repent & be baptized 3. One is coming]*
2. What are the main elements of Jesus' message? *[handwritten: 1. K. has come. 2. K. is still coming 3. I am the way]*
3. What elements of John's message are included in Jesus' message? *[handwritten: Repent & be baptized]*
4. What new messages are revealed in Jesus' preaching? *[handwritten: All 3.]*

Questions for Discussion

1. How do you think the people of John's day felt when they heard his proclamation that the kingdom of heaven was at hand?

2. If the kingdom of God and the kingdom of heaven are to be regarded as two different kings, does this change our understanding of Jesus' message? In what way?

3. If the Old Testament people of God found the forgiveness of sins through repentance, why were they required to offer up sacrifices?

4. List ways in which our own times are like those of Jesus. *[handwritten: K. coming / J. is the way]*

5. How is our situation—in terms of God's redemption—like the situation of the people in Jesus' time? *[handwritten: We live now in K. age.]*

4

THE PRESENT KINGDOM

Biblical Texts: Isaiah 40:1-5; 61:1-6; Luke 3:1-20; 4:16-21

Isaiah 40:1-5 and 61:1-6 are prophecies of Isaiah regarding Israel's hope for the future.
In Luke 3:1-20 there is an account of John the Baptist's ministry in which the prophecies of Isaiah are referred to.
Luke 4:16-21 is an account of the beginning of Christ's ministry in which he claims to be fulfilling the prophecies of Isaiah.

John the Baptist and Jesus both began their ministries by proclaiming that the kingdom of heaven was at hand. Their preaching had a sort of urgency which is often lacking in preaching today. It also had a broad scope which preaching today does not always take on. The sense of urgency and broad scope was due to the message concerning the arrival of the kingdom of heaven.

There are three things concerning the kingdom of heaven which are important to us here:

1. The kingdom of heaven was something which the Old Testament people of God were looking forward to.
2. The kingdom of heaven came with Jesus Christ.
3. The arrival of the kingdom of heaven has implications for today, because we live in the time period of its arrival.

The Kingdom of Heaven in the Old Testament

The phrase "kingdom of heaven" occurs only rarely in the Old Testament. Yet we can see that the Old Testament people of God possessed a hope for the future. This hope for the future figures in the proclamation of the arrival of the kingdom by John and Jesus. In Isaiah 40:1-5 we see certain aspects of this hope.

1. First of all we see that part of the hope of the Old Testament people was the hope of deliverance from war. While in our own times there have been anti-war movements, what is expressed in Isaiah is something quite different. It is the longing of a people who were often oppressed by war. Their cities had been surrounded by the enemy. They had to live in the cramped quarters of these ancient near-eastern cities for months at a time without anyone going out or coming in. Disease and starvation brought suffering and death to the people. As expressed by Isaiah, the people had the hope that one day their hard service would be completed, and their sins would be paid for. This last phrase indicates the underlying assumption that they were suffering because of sin, but they hoped that one day they would receive forgiveness for these sins.

2. The second hope we see expressed in Isaiah is that one day the glory of the Lord would be revealed. This hope is tied to the former. The reason they would find relief from war would be because the glory of the Lord would appear. By glory, Isaiah meant that God himself would appear.

We find additional aspects of this hope of God's Old Testament people in Isaiah 61:1-6. Here we see that the coming time would be one of great prosperity. It would be a time of happiness rather than a time of despair. It will be a time of rebuilding and shepherding and farming. And it would be a time when God's people would enjoy the wealth of the nations.

Isaiah said that God's spirit was on him—that he was anointed to preach good news to the poor. This good news to the poor was that just such a time of peace and prosperity was coming.

The Kingdom of Heaven Came With Jesus

The message of John and Jesus is that this period of peace and prosperity which the Old Testament people of God had looked forward to has arrived. In their preaching they quoted the words of Isaiah as applying to themselves in their own time.

In Luke 3:1-6 John says that he is the one who is crying to prepare the way of the Lord because his glory is coming. John substitutes the word salvation for God's glory perhaps because he saw this as the time when sins would be forgiven and people would no more have to suffer for their sins.

In Luke 4:16-19 Christ applies some of the words of Isaiah to himself. On the occasion of his being chosen to read in the synagogue service, Christ says that the prophecy of Isaiah is fulfilled in himself. The custom of the Jews was and still is that seven people are chosen to read in a synagogue service. It was probably in this normal course of events that Jesus' turn to read came. By coincidence—or rather divine plan—the passage Christ read was this passage from Isaiah. He read it and then sat down to speak.

Jesus proclaims that this prophecy of Isaiah was fulfilled in their hearing. Needless to say this was not the sort of sermon which the Jews were used to hearing. Many ancient sermons of the Jewish Rabbis have survived in the Jewish "Midrash," but none of them begin with the proclamation of the fulfillment of prophecy.

Considering this prophecy which Christ says was fulfilled in him, we see three important things about the kingdom of heaven which he proclaimed: *1) it is a time of salvation, 2) it is a time of healing and 3) it is a time of blessing.*

- *1) It is a time of salvation.* Jesus says it is a time to preach good news to the poor—to proclaim freedom for the prisoners. As we saw in Isaiah, the Old Testament people of God looked forward to a time when they would no longer suffer for their sins. Jesus is proclaiming that with his coming this time has arrived. This is in agreement with other things which Christ said and explains their significance. On one occasion (Matthew 9:1-8) Jesus said to a paralytic man, "Your sins are forgiven." The Pharisees criticized this statement by asking who can forgive sins but God. Jesus replied, "Which is easier: to say, 'Yours sins are forgiven,' or to say 'Get up and walk'?" Then he told the paralytic man to get up and walk. When that man stood up and walked, he demonstrated Christ's power to heal and his power to forgive sins. Christ's message included the proclamation that he was able to forgive sins.

- 2) *It is a time of healing*. When Christ said recovery of sight for the blind, this could be understood as referring to spiritual blindness. Living according to this present sinful world was often likened to being blind. Yet, when we consider how often Jesus actually healed blind people, we cannot help but consider the fact that in some sense Jesus meant this literally. When sin entered the world through Adam, many problems also entered as a part of the curse of sin. When Jesus came and offered salvation—the forgiveness of sins as an end to suffering because of sin—he did not limit this work to a mere psychological relief. Just as Christ brought the forgiveness of sins he brought relief from suffering—the recovery of sight to the blind.

- 3) *It is a time of blessing*. Jesus says it is the Year of the Lord's favor. In the passage of Isaiah from which this quotation comes, the year of the Lord's favor was the time when the ancient cities would be rebuilt, the time of shepherding, and the time of harvesting. We seldom think of them as such, but some of the miracles of Christ offer proof that Christ saw this as one of the results of his coming. There is the miracle of the feeding of the five thousand, and the miracle of the many fishes. These miracles show that Christ is able to give great physical prosperity.

Jesus proclaimed that the hope and expectations of the Old Testament people of God were fulfilled in him. He proclaimed this present reality of the fulfillment of prophecy as the coming of the kingdom of God.

The Kingdom of Heaven Today

One thing that we must realize concerning Christ's proclamation is that it holds true for our day as well. We live in the age after the appearance of Christ. Christ came and accomplished his work. He ascended on high to sit at the right hand of the Father, he said that he was going to prepare a place for us, and that he would come again. But in all this one fact remains: we do not live in the age of expectation—as the Old Testament people of God did—but rather we live in the age of the reality. <u>The kingdom has come! It is a present reality</u>.

We may sum up the implication of the present reality of the kingdom under three headings: *1) Today is the day of salvation, 2) Today is the day of healing, and 3) Today is the day of blessing.*

- The church has been most aware of the reality that <u>*today is the day of salvation*</u>. We recognize that we can find salvation—forgiveness of sins—now, and we proclaim this salvation to the world. We command everyone to repent of sins, to look to God through Jesus Christ for the forgiveness of sins, and to afterward live holy lives.

- The two remaining implications—that <u>*today is the day of healing and the day of blessing*</u>—have not occupied the efforts of the church of Christ nearly so much as the reality of salvation. These are, nevertheless, concerns of Christ's people. At the creation God gave men the work of subduing the earth and ruling over the creatures (<u>Genesis 1:28</u>). When sin entered into the world, many hardships also entered, but God did not take away from man this work of subduing and ruling. When Christ came he commanded his disciples to go and preach the gospel, but he did not take away from them the work of subduing and ruling. The bringing of healing and blessing to mankind is part of this work of subduing the earth and ruling over it.

The disciples were empowered with supernatural gifts and performed miracles which included healing and extraordinary means of communicating the gospel. We today do not share the supernatural gifts for communicating the gospel such as prophecy and tongues, but we still participate in this work of taking the message of Jesus Christ to all the world. It seems that <u>we should not shrink from the work of bringing healing and prosperity merely because we do not possess supernatural gifts for such</u>. Today we have the completed Scriptures and the work of the Holy Spirit to assist us in this work.

Conclusion

The Message of John the Baptist and Jesus was that the kingdom of God was at hand—their message had a <u>sense of urgency</u>. Today the kingdom has come—yes, in some senses it is still coming, and we will consider this in the next chapter—but our message today ought also to have a sense of urgency for we are engaged in the work of Christ.

The message of Christ also had implications for all creation. We must be engaged in the work of the proclamation of the gospel which Jesus brought, but we must never forget that the work of the kingdom is also that of bringing healing and prosperity. <u>We must not think that only those who preach and teach are engaged in the work of the kingdom.</u>

We see thousands perishing in sins and going to an eternity of retribution, and we are moved to action. Today there are thousands dying of starvation, and thousands dying of diseases for which there are cures. Ought we not to be moved with a sense of urgency to act in all aspects of the kingdom work of Jesus Christ?

Questions for Review

1. What future expectations were included in the hope of God's Old Testament people? *deliverance from war, forgiveness of sins; G's glory;* — *Isa. 40* ← ↓ — *Isa. 61 - great prosperity.*

2. What three important things did Jesus proclaim about the kingdom of heaven? *time of salvation, healing, + blessing*

3. What are three implications of the present reality of the kingdom of heaven? *same as #2*

4. How does the teaching of Christ regarding the present significance of the kingdom of heaven develop ideas contained in the message of John the Baptist? *urgency; forgiveness → action; breadth of Kingdom*

Questions for Discussion

1. In this chapter three aspects of the kingdom are mentioned: salvation, healing, and blessing. Is the church to be actively engaged in bringing about all three aspects?

2. The disciples were empowered with supernatural gifts for their work in the kingdom. Is the church today empowered with such gifts?

3. If you feel that the work of the church includes bringing healing, but that the church is not empowered with supernatural gifts, how does the church bring about healing? If the work of the church does not include healing, but you feel that the church is empowered with supernatural gifts, why are such gifts given?

4. Discuss the various possible combinations of views raised by the previous questions and what conclusions they lead to.

5

THE GROWING KINGDOM

Biblical Text: Matthew 13:31-33

Matthew 13:31-33 contains two parables of Jesus. These are the parables of the mustard seed and the parable of the leaven or yeast.

In the previous chapter, we saw how the kingdom of God was clearly something which was arriving in the days of John the Baptist and Jesus. But despite the fact that the kingdom of God was something present to John and Jesus, it had aspects which were ongoing. The ongoing aspects of the coming of the kingdom may be seen in the parables of the mustard seed and the leaven, to which we will now turn our attention.

In trying to understand these parables, we must first answer the basic question: How do we generally interpret parables? There are three basic principles which apply here.

1. Always seek to understand the parable in the way it was intended to be understood.

Jesus spoke in parables to communicate some truth about God and his kingdom. When we seek to understand the parable, what we are looking for is the particular truth that was intended. This truth is usually something that can be stated as a sentence. Another way of referring to this truth is to call it the *theme* of the parable. The first step in seeking to understand any parable, then, is to ask what is the theme of the parable.

2. Look for the interpretation of the parable in the Scriptures themselves.

Very often Jesus explained his parables. In these cases we sometimes find the theme of the parable in a statement Jesus made to the disciples. When Jesus does not explain his parables, it is still very often the case that the meaning of the parable can be determined from the context in which the parable is found. In any case, since we recognize the unity of the Scriptures, we know that what we find as the theme of the parable will not be something that contradicts what the Scriptures teach elsewhere.

3. Be careful not to see meaning where there is none.

In trying to understand a parable, people sometimes get misled by thinking that the parable says more than it really does. In the parable of the sower (Matthew 13:1-9), for example, how much significance does the sower's sack have? Or his cloak? Not every little detail of the event which is described in the parable must have meaning.

The Theme of the Parables

In our parables we want to find out what the theme is. Both of these parables begin, "The kingdom of heaven is like . . .." If we want to understand these parables we must understand how these two things are alike: a mustard seed and yeast. What is it that these two things have in common? They are both very small living organisms but which have very great results. The little tiny grain of mustard seed becomes a great tree. The leaven or yeast is put into the barrel of flour and its affects the whole measure of flour. These are small things which have a very great effect. But also, they have this great effect and this great growth because they are living organisms.

Also, single?

May we not conclude from these observations that the theme of these parables is three-fold? First of all, the kingdom as a living organism has a life giving source. Secondly, the kingdom is an

The Mustard Seed and Plant
(Brassica nigra)

3. organic whole. And thirdly, its growth to maturity is inevitable.

First, the kingdom has a life giving source. The parable is about a mustard seed and yeast. A dry roasted peanut would not have the same effect. Nor would a freeze-dried, refried, organically-grown bean from the organic food store. It has to be a seed that is capable of germination. It has to be something that is living to give life. When you go to the store and buy yeast, you always turn the package over to look at the expiration date. After that date the yeast will not raise the dough. It has to be living, life giving yeast.

The kingdom of God, this parable says, must have a life giving source. It must draw from a life giving source. The implication is that the source of the kingdom is none other than Jesus Christ himself. Christ indicated this in his ministry. When he spoke to the disciples, he said, "I am the way, and the truth, and the life (John 14:6)." When he spoke to the woman at the well in Samaria, he said, "If you knew the gift of God and who it is that asks you for a drink, you would have asked him and he would have given you living water (John 4:10 NIV)."

After Christ's ascension, the apostles taught concerning the exalted Christ that he was the life giving source of the kingdom. In I Corinthians 15:45, Paul comparing Christ with Adam says, 'So it is written: "The first man Adam became a living being": the last Adam, a life-giving spirit.' In Romans 8:10 we also read, "But if Christ is in you, your body is dead because of sin, yet your spirit is alive because of righteousness. And if the Spirit of him who raised up Jesus from the dead is living in you, he who raised Christ from the dead will also give life to your mortal bodies through his Spirit, who lives in you (NIV)."

Christ is the life giving source of the kingdom. He is the life source of every believer. He is the life source of the church. It is our responsibility to ask if we are part of that kingdom drawing from the life giving source. Jesus, speaking to the disciples about the vine and the branches, said that all those dead branches—those branches which are not drawing life from the vine—will be cut off and cast out. If we are not drawing from this life giving source of the kingdom of Jesus

Christ, we must, as Christ said to the woman at the well in Samaria, ask that he might give us living water. We must say, as she did, "Sir, give me this water."

Secondly, the kingdom of God grows as an organic whole. In these parables, the kingdom of God is not compared to a bucket of seed that was scattered about and a whole orchard grew from it. It is not compared unto several little cakes of yeast, each one put into a loaf of bread or rolls. Rather, it is illustrated by one mustard seed. It is illustrated by one bit of leaven that affects the whole barrel. The kingdom of Jesus Christ, the kingdom of God is an organic whole.

The unity of the kingdom is the expressed desire and prayer of Jesus Christ. We see this if we look at John 17:20. The passage in which this verse appears is often referred to as the high priestly prayer of Jesus Christ. It is the prayer which he is praying as he foresees his coming crucifixion. He says this regarding the disciples, "My prayer is not for them alone. I pray also for those who will believe in me through their message, that all of them may be one, Father, just as you are in me and I am in you. May they also be in us so that the world may believe that you have sent me (John 17:20-21 NIV)."

Christ knew that there would be Baptists and Presbyterians, Congregationalists, Brethren In Christ, Mennonites, etc. Christ knew that the church would be divided, continually disagreeing over points of doctrine. His prayer was, may they all be one even as Father and Son are one.

It is important to now notice two things about this prayer. He does not say, "Father, all those that agree to baptize believers by immersion, let them be one, and those that baptize infants, let them be one." Christ prays for all those who believe in him through the testimony of the disciples—may they be one. We must have such a desire for unity with all our Christian brethren.

Also notice that Christ says, "For those who will believe in me through their message." He does not call for unity with those who do not believe the testimony of the disciples—the Christian gospel of the Scriptures. He does not call for unity with those who have other testimonies—perhaps the *Book of Mormon* or the writings of Mary Baker Eddy. But Christ prays for unity of all those who believe through the message of the disciples. This is Christ's prayer and it ought to be ours also.

Finally, the kingdom of God, just as the leaven and just as the mustard seed, grew to maturity. The leaven affected the whole measure of flour, and the mustard seed grew to be a great tree. It is not a parable about an elm seed that was put into the ground and it grew to be a great big spreading elm tree. What shade trees elms can be! But in time it became infected with the Dutch Elm disease and it was good for nothing but to cut down and use for firewood. The kingdom is not compared to the lady who took yeast, put it in the flour, mixed it up and made bread. She put it in the oven but a high speed jet came over and made a sonic boom. The bread fell, and it was good for nothing but to pull out and throw away. The parable says, that the seed will grow to be a great tree. It says that the leaven will leaven all the flour.

These parables have an optimistic outlook for the kingdom of heaven. And this optimistic outlook has caused a lot of problems to some Bible students and Bible scholars alike. To some it seems inconsistent with what Christ said in Luke 17:26 that in the last days it will be as in the days of Noah. It seems inconsistent with what we have heard preachers preach from the book of Revelation. Often the church at Laodicea, which is lukewarm and will be spit out, is said to be what the church will be like in the last days. The Scriptures also tell us about great tribulation and persecution of the church in the last days. How then do these parables tell us that the kingdom of heaven will grow to be a great tree whose branches fill the air—that it will be like leaven that leavens every bit of flour in the dough.[1]

These parables are optimistic with respect to the kingdom of heaven. It will grow to be a great tree, it will affect the whole flour. But we really should not have any problem with the otpimism of these parables, because both the teaching of a victorious church and the teaching of apostasy and persecution are biblical doctrines.

Perhaps you have heard terms such as pretribulatonism, premillennialism, postmillennialism, and amillennialism. We do not need to enter into this debate here to solve our problem. What is important is that we understand <u>two strains of teaching that are running through the Scriptures with respect to the end times.</u> One strain is that Satan and the powers of Satan will fight against the church. As the end times come nearer, seeing their doom, they will fight all the more viciously and vigorously. Yet at the same time, it is the clear teaching of the Scriptures—as in these parables—that the kingdom of heaven will be victorious. How can this be?

We may possibly have an explanation when we realize that many times <u>the struggle between the Satanic powers and the people of God is compared to warfare.</u> If we follow this analogy, we can understand how it is that both of these teachings of Scripture can be true. Those who remember the <u>Second World War</u> may remember that as the allied forces landed at Normandy and pressed closer and closer to the German heartland some of the most pitched battles of the war were fought. The Battle of the Bulge was fought as the war was nearing an end. Seeing their doom, the Germany Army made a last valiant effort, but the victory belonged to the allies. The outcome of the war had become evident at Normandy. In the Pacific island hopping campaign, as the allied forces moved closer and closer towards the heartland of Japan, battles took place such as that on Iwo Jima where the enemy had to literally be burned out of the caves and crevices of the rocks. But again the outcome of the war had become evident.

This is the way it is in the warfare between spiritual darkness and the kingdom of heaven. <u>The victory is God's.</u> The victory belongs to the people of God. As we press on toward the end of the ages, and that victory becomes more and more certain, <u>with its last ounce of strength the kingdom of spiritual darkness will strike out</u> even more viciously than ever before. But the kingdom *will* be a great tree, and the yeast *will* affect that whole measure of flour.

<u>This parable does not teach that all will be saved.</u> The tree does not <u>fill the air.</u> The leaven does not make the <u>flour turn into leaven.</u> Yet, it is a great tree whose branches stretch into the sky and spread out, and the yeast affects every nook and cranny of that bowl of flour and

leavens it all. It will be the case, just as Christ has promised in Revelation 7:9, where the vision is of a great multitude which no man can number of all nations, and kindreds, and people, and tongues. They will stand before the throne and say with a loud voice, "Salvation belongs to our God, who sits upon the throne, and to the Lamb."

The Kingdom is Coming

One important thing to be learned from these parables, which applies to our desire to understand the overall message of the New Testament, is that the kingdom is still coming. In the previous chapter we saw that the kingdom came with Jesus, but in this chapter we see that in at least one sense it is still coming—it is still growing to maturity.

We must realize, however, that it is one kingdom, one work of God, which is an on-going process. It began with Christ's coming, continues as he is in his exalted state, and will consumate with the events that surround his return.

[1]Alternate interpretations of these parables usually attempt to make these parables a picture of growing apostasy in the church. Such an interpretation is found in the *Scofield Chain Reference Bible*. Here Scofield objects to interpreting the leaven parable as teaching that the world will be converted in this age (which is not what this author is saying). His objection to this interpretation, however, is based on some inadequate observations. First, he notes that leaven usually represents sin, this does not preclude leaven being used to illustrate something else. In this parable it is stated, "The kingdom of heaven is like unto leaven (Authorized Version)." It would be nonsense to say this means, "The kingdom of heaven is like sin." Secondly, Scofield objects to the idea of a converted world, and rightly so. But such is not the only alternative interpetation of the parable. Thirdly, he sees the *mingling* of the leaven by a *woman* as significant of corruption. This argument is again based on usage of such figures elsewhere, and as with the use of leaven, does not preclude their signifying something else here. Regarding these objects we may again state that it is important that the parable be interpreted as it was intended, and in a manner which supports scriptural teaching elsewhere.

Regarding the parable of the mustard seed, Scofield has less to say. He regards this parable as a picture of rapid but unsubstantial growth. What must be noted is that in the parable itself the emphasis is not on the weak character of the tree, but on its greatness: "It is the greatest among herbs (Authorized Version)."

Questions for Review

1. What are the future aspects of the kingdom? *[handwritten: life-giving source; grows as an organic whole; grows to maturity]*

2. Compare the future aspects of the kingdom with the present aspects. *[handwritten: salvation-thru Xt   healing-wholeness   blessing-expanse, growth]*

6. Why do we speak of one kingdom with present and future aspects rather than two kingdoms: one present and one future? *[handwritten: one seed, one leaven lump]*

4. Do you think that the interpretation of the parables of the mustard seed and the yeast given in this chapter are correct? Why or why not?

Questions for Discussion

1. In this chapter, three principles were given for interpreting parables. Do you think that there are other principles which should have been included?

2. Christ prayed for unity among believers. Why don't all believers unite into one church?

3. How do various eschatological views relate to the interpretation, given in this chapter, of the parables of the mustard seed and the yeast?

4. What eschatological view do you feel the author has favored? Which view do you favor?

5. Can Christians with various views of the future work together?

6

THE COMING JUDGMENT

Biblical Text: Luke 17:20-37

In Luke 17:20-37 Jesus responds to the question, "When will the kingdom come?" He responds by saying it does not come visibly. It is among you. Jesus then teaches regarding the terrible times that are yet to come.

In chapter four, we saw that Jesus taught that the kingdom of God had come. In this chapter he is asked when the kingdom of God will come. Apparently the Pharisee who asked this question had been absent when Jesus answered the Beelzebub charge by saying if he cast out demons by the Spirit of God, then the kingdom of God had already come. Jesus responds to this question quite tactfully pointing out the invisible character of the present aspect of the kingdom. But then he goes on to affirm the fact that the kingdom has already arrived by saying that the kingdom of God is among you.[1]

If we think back over the things we considered in chapter four, we realize that the present aspects of the kingdom are quite invisible. Even though some effects of the kingdom's having come may be seen in the world, the sort of kingdom which the Pharisees apparently anticipated was not what Christ would have them look for. Jesus then turns to his disciples and describes a quite visible aspect of the kingdom that is still future—judgment.

In the previous chapter, we saw how the kingdom's growth to maturity is a future aspect of the kingdom. In this passage we see that judgment is also a future aspect of the kingdom.

The Present and Future Kingdom

Present Aspects
-Salvation
-Healing
-Blessing

Future Aspects
-Growth to Fullness
-Judgment

The Coming Judgment

In this passage on the coming judgment, Jesus indicates four aspects of this judgment for our consideration. The coming judgment will be:

1) unexpected,
2) swift and terrible,
3) thorough, and
4) final

The coming judgment will be <u>unexpected</u>

Jesus uses two historical allusions to illustrate the unexpected character of the coming judgment. He says it will be like the day of Noah (Genesis 7) and the day of Lot (Genesis 19). In these times people were eating and drinking. We sometimes think this means they were being gluttonous and drunken, but it probably does not mean this. It also says they were being married and given in marriage, buying and selling, and planting and building, and none of these activities are particularly sinful. Eating and drinking, therefore, probably means that <u>life was going on as usual.</u> The days of Noah and Lot were particularly sinful times, but what is being emphasized here is not so much the sinfulness of the days as the suddenness of judgment which came at those times. It was a surprise to the people of those days, and so will the coming judgment be for the people of a future day.

The coming judgment will be swift and terrible

When that day comes, says Jesus, the one who is on his roof should not go inside to get his goods. Being on the roof was quite normal in those days as it was sort of an upstairs patio. The one in the field should not go back for anything. So quickly will the day come. vv. 31-33

The unpredictability of the coming judgment and its swiftness is frightening in itself, but the judgment is frightening for other reasons as well. It will be like the deluge. It will be like the fire and sulfur which rained down on Sodom. The person who tries to keep his life will lose it.

The coming judgment will be thorough and final

The last part of this text is often used to describe the rapture of the saints—to show what will happen when Christ returns. The ones taken are said to be those who are caught up in the air to meet Christ as Paul describes this event in I Thessalonians 4:17. But there are a couple of problems with this view. vv. 34-37

First, the passage is about judgment. It does not mention anything about a return of Christ. Jesus' disciples would not likely understand any teaching about Christ's return at this point in his ministry since they, at this point, do not even know of his death and resurrection. Secondly, the disciples respond to hearing that these people will be taken with the question, "Where?" Not where will they be left, but where will they be taken. The disciples know where those who are left will be left. They will be left in bed and grinding grain. In answer to the question, Christ replies, "Where there is a dead body, there the vultures will gather." This could hardly refer to the raptured saints. 1. 2.

The exact meaning of this passage is unclear. But it is clear that this passage teaches that judgment is coming. That judgment will be unexpected, swift and terrible, and it will be thorough and final. The thorough character of judgment is seen in the reference to people being taken whether grinding grain or in bed. The final character is seen in the references to death—especially of those being taken to where the vultures are gathered.

The Message of Christ in Review

We must remember at this point that we have only studied Christ's message as he taught it to the disciples in his life on earth. It would be a mistake to think that anything else that was said about Jesus later by other writers of the New Testament is somehow secondary in nature. What Christ taught was what the disciples were able to comprehend at the time—they even had trouble understanding parts of what he taught then. It was after the death, resurrection, and ascension that the disciples came to understand more fully the significance of his life and deeds.

At this point we do need to gather together the various aspects of what Christ did teach. We may summarize the message of Christ at this point as follows:

1. The Kingdom has come
   a. The time of salvation
   b. The time of healing   *"already"*
   c. The time of blessing
2. The Kingdom is still coming
   a. It will grow to fullness   *"not yet"*
   b. Judgment is still coming
3. I am the way.   *unifying principle ("all the promises...are yes...in X-t")*

We may say that Jesus taught that the great day which was expected—the kingdom of heaven—had arrived. It had arrived and was still arriving. It had arrived because of one person—Jesus himself. Jesus is the one who brought in the kingdom age. He was the Davidic king which was expected. He was the Messiah. He was God himself who had come to his holy temple.

The Deeds of Jesus

Up to this point our study of Jesus has focused primarily on what Jesus said, almost to the exclusion of studying what Jesus did. If one were to ask, "Which is more important—what Jesus said or what Jesus did?" one would be asking one of those which-came-first questions. What Jesus did was: *He accomplished the redemption of God's people*. The accomplishment of redemption was through his deeds. Deeds which it is more correct to speak about as a complex act: the death-crucifixion-ascension act. It was Jesus' teaching which revealed to lost mankind that this redemption was accomplished through Jesus the Messiah.

In a biblical-theological study, we are primarily concerned with the unfolding of revelation. We do not dwell at length on theological questions such as, why Christ died, or how Christ's death accomplished redemption. These are legitimate studies in their own right, but belong more to the realm of systematic studies than biblical-theological studies.

[margin: O.T. "former prophets"]

Appropriate to a biblical-theological study, however, is the question: What do the acts of Jesus reveal? What do they add to our knowledge of God's dealing with mankind? The answer to these questions is: They reveal that Jesus is the Way! They are the testimony—the proof—to the third point of Jesus' message that he is the one who accomplishes the hope of God's people. Under the Old Testament, that hope was that redemption would be accomplished in some future work of God. Jesus' message is that he accomplished that work. His deeds accomplished it. Under the New Testament, the hope of his people is future glorificaton through the historic work of God—Jesus' deeds.

[margin: Ro.1 / I Cor.15 / more later.]

Old and New Perspective

Future Hope Based On Future Work →	Future Hope Based On ← Historic Work
Old Testament	New Testament

---

[1] I think the translation in the footnote of the NIV is more accurate than the translation in the text.

Questions for Review

1. What are the present and what are the future aspects of the kingdom?

2. Name four characteristics of the coming judgment.

3. Why did Jesus use the days of Noah and the days of Lot to describe what the last days will be like?

4. What are the basic elements of the message of Christ?

Questions for Discussion

1. Is it possible to correctly say that what Jesus did is more important than what he said?

2. In this chapter the coming judgment is described as unexpected. Does this mean that Christ's return will be unpredictable?

3. Will the coming judgment be unexpected for all? Will it be a judgment for God's people?

4. Discuss some of the questions raised in the last part of this chapter: Why did Christ die? How did his death accomplish the redemption of his people?

7

THE PREACHING OF THE APOSTLES

Biblical Texts: Acts 2:14–41; 7:1–53; 13:13–43

> *Acts 2:14–41 contains the sermon of Peter on the Day of Pentecost.*
> *Acts 7:1 53 contains Stephen's speech to the Sanhedrin.*
> *Acts 13:13–43 contains the sermon of Paul at Pisidian Antioch.*

We have seen that John the Baptist's message was one that pointed to Christ. We have seen that Christ's message was one that pointed to himself as the one who brings in the kingdom of heaven. As we go on from the teachings of Christ to those of his apostles, we find that the message of the apostles pointed back to Jesus. We also find a fundamentally different character to the preaching of the apostles, which sets it off from the preaching of John and Jesus. The messages of the apostles are expositions of the Old Testament.

John and Jesus spoke of fulfilling the Old Testament. It is recorded that Jesus explained how the whole Old Testament spoke of him (Luke 24:27). We do not, however, have a record of what Jesus said when he explained the Scriptures. With the ascension of Jesus and the beginning of apostolic preaching, we find that the book of Acts records how the apostles explained the Old Testament as speaking of Jesus. It seems likely that the method of the apostles was learned from Jesus. It is profitable for us to spend some time looking at these apostolic sermons as evidence of how the Old Testament speaks of Christ.

Apostolic Preaching

On the day of Pentecost, we are told, the Holy Spirit came upon the apostles. After this happened, men of various nations heard the apostles speaking in their own language. Their amazement at this prompts Peter to stand up and comment on the situation with a sermon (Acts 2:14-41).

Peter's Sermon

When this sermon is printed in such a manner as to emphasize the portions which are Old Testament quotations, it becomes evident immediately that the sermon consists largely of three Old Testament quotations. *The New International Version* sets off the Old Testament quotations by setting up the lines as lines of poetry. *The New American Standard Bible* sets the Old Testament quotations in capital letters. The sermon, as recorded, consists mainly of these quotations. While the actual sermon delivered on that day may have been longer, Luke's representation of it in Acts is likely a condensed version which displays what the sermon's pattern was.

The first of these quotations is a quotation of Joel 2:28-32, and it is contained in Acts 2:17-21. This prophecy of Joel is about the last days. Peter says that what was happening there in Jerusalem on the day of Pentecost was what the prophet Joel had spoken about when he made this prophecy.

The second quotation is found in Acts 2:25-28, and it is a quotation of Psalm 16:8-11. This passage speaks of God's promise of eternal life to his "Holy One." The Holy One will neither be abandoned to the grave nor see decay. Peter says that when David wrote this Psalm he was speaking of the resurrection of Christ.

The third quotation in Acts 2:34-35 is also a Psalm of David. This Psalm is sometimes confusing to readers. The phrase, "The Lord said to my Lord," seems nonsensical to some. What has to be realized here is that in the Hebrew original of the Psalm, the first and second words translated "Lord" are different Hebrew words. The first word is the name of God, "Yahweh." The second word is the word "lord."

"My lord" means "me." A more intelligible translation of the Psalm then is: "Yahweh said to me."

Peter says that in Psalm 110:1 David was talking about the ascension of Christ. He says that when David says "me," he does not mean David, but he is writing the Psalm as though it were the Messiah speaking. Peter says that the Psalm means: "Yahweh said to the Messiah, 'Sit at my right hand.'"

Stephen's Speech

In Acts 6:8-15, we read how Stephen was a man full of God's grace and who did great wonders. He was opposed, however, by members of a particular synagogue who accused him of blasphemy and brought him before the court (the Sanhedrin). Acts 7:1-53 contains Stephen's speech to the Sanhedrin.

Stephen's speech begins as a history of Israel. Stephen is explaining things which the members of the Sanhedrin knew well enough themselves. In this speech, Stephen is emphasizing that God has been at work in Israel's history. At the point in the story where Solomon built the temple, Stephen departs from this history to make a theological point—God does not dwell in a temple made with human hands. Stephen was implying that one finds the true worship of God in a spiritual worship and not in the Jerusalem temple. This aroused the anger of the Sanhedrin.

Paul's Sermon

At Pisidian Antioch, Paul, in a manner similar to Stephen's, tells the history of Israel (Acts 13:16-41). When he gets to David, he makes a connection with Jesus. Jesus, says Paul, is David's Son. Paul then gives several quotations from the Old Testament.

The first quotation is from Psalm 2:7 (Acts 13:33). This was a Psalm about the Davidic kingship. Paul says it is about Jesus. Paul also quotes Psalm 16:10 (Acts 13:35), another Davidic Psalm, as being about Jesus.

In verse 41, Paul quotes Habakkuk 1:5 as a word of warning.

People should not fail to believe as people in Habakkuk's day had failed to believe, says Paul.

One final quotation which needs to be seen is in verse 35. This is a quotation from Isaiah 55:3. Isaiah 55:3 was a promise of God given by Isaiah to describe the then future glory of restored Israel. This verse Paul says is also about Jesus.

The Apostolic Use of the Old Testament

After looking at these three sermons, we should make some general observations regarding the ways the apostles understood and used the Old Testament.

Old Testament Prophecies Fulfilled

When the passage in the Old Testament is about a future day, the apostles understood this future day as being their day. This is what Peter is saying when he quotes Joel 2:28-32. He says the times of which Joel spoke are now here. Paul also, when he quotes from Isaiah 55:3, is saying that the future days of which Isaiah spoke are now here.

The prophecies of the Old Testament contain many references to a future day when God—Yahweh in the Old Testament—would restore Israel, bring in a time of peace and prosperity, blessing on the nations, and judgment on the enemies of God. The Old Testament prophecies seem to portray all of these events as one great day of Yahweh.

The message of the apostles is that that day has arrived. The prophecies of Joel, Isaiah and others are being fulfilled.

The Old Testament Types

When the apostles speak about David and about Solomon's temple, there is a different use of the Old Testament. In the Psalms of the Old Testament, we find David speaking about Christ—or do we?

David was speaking about David first and foremost. God had

made promises to David in II Samuel 7. We saw in the second chapter of this book that these promises were the basis of Jewish expectations for a future Davidic king. Since God had made promises to David regarding his future son, then when David spoke about himself and God's goodness to him, he was also speaking of the future king—the Messiah. As God established David, so God would establish the Messiah.

When the Old Testament is understood by the apostles in this manner, it is called typology. <u>The apostles understood the Old Testament to have double references to its own day and the future messianic age.</u> This use of typology was not the invention of the apostles. We saw an example of this in chapter two in the quote from Qumran of a commentary on II Samuel 7. Such commentaries are referred to as *pesher*.

Pesher

Pesher is a type of biblical commentary which was prevalent before and during Christ's time. It is found in the Dead Sea scrolls and other Jewish writings, and it is clearly the way the apostles commented on the Old Testament. Pesher assumes that:

1. The whole Old Testament reveals eternal truths.
2. The true meaning of the Old Testament is to be found in the messianic events of the last days.
3. The events and persons of the Old Testament relate to the events and persons of the messianic age as type-antetype. (Shamgar, i.e.)

Recognizing this manner of understanding the Old Testament, we see more clearly <u>what it means that Jesus "fulfilled" the law and the prophets</u>. This does not mean that every passage of the Old Testament was a predictive passage in a literal sense. Rather it is often the case that the Old Testament passage is regarded by the New Testament writer to have been a prophetic picture of the Messiah and that Jesus is believed to be the one pictured.

When the twofold aspect of the Old Testament as <u>predictive-prophecy and picture-prophecy is seen</u>, (1), (2) ! it is clearer how Jesus fulfilled *all* the law and the prophets.

67

Use of the Old Testament Today

As we know well, the Old Testament is God's word. The message of the Old Testament is important to us today just as it was to the apostles. Sometimes we hear preaching from the Old Testament today which regards it as predictive prophecy. The prophecies are sometimes regarded as predictive of events that are still future or of events that are soon to pass.

In the message of the apostles, however, <u>the predictive aspects of the Old Testament</u> are seen differently. Th<u>ey are seen primarily in terms of how they portray Christ</u>. We would do well to also understand the Old Testament primarily as it teaches us about Christ.

Questions for Review

1. What is a good text to show how the apostles used the Old Testament?
2. What are three ways the apostles used the Old Testament? (1) fulfilment (2) typology (3) pesher
3. What are three characteristics of pesher?
4. Did Jesus use the Old Testament in the same way that the apostles did?
5. In what way is Christ central to the message of the apostles?

Questions for Discussion

1. This chapter mentions three ways that the apostles use the Old Testament. Are there other ways besides these in which the apostles use the Old Testament?

2. Is it right for Christians today to interpret the Old Testament typologically where the New Testament has not done so?

3. This chapter states three principles involved in pesher. Are these principles stated anywhere in the New Testament? Are statements made in the New Testament which might indicate that these principles are generally held?

4. David is referred to in this chapter as a type of Christ. Were other Old Testament characters typological of Christ?

An Exercise In Understanding How The New Testament Uses The Old

The following is a list of passages from the New Testament which may be quoting or referring to passages we have considered. Read the Old Testament passages first and answer the question, "What is this talking about?" Then read the New Testament passage and answer the question, "What is this talking about?" Then answer the question, "How does the New Testament writer use the Old Testament?" Does he use it as an illustration, as a proof text, as allegory, or how?

Deuteronomy 32:35	Luke 21:22
Deuteronomy 32:35	Romans 12:19
Deuteronomy 32:36	Hebrews 10:30
Deuteronomy 32:40	Revelation 10:5-6
Deuteronomy 32:43	Romans 15:10
Deuteronomy 32:43	Revelation 6:10
Deuteronomy 32:43	Revelation 19:2
II Samuel 7:14	II Corinthians 6:18
II Samuel 7:14	Hebrews 1:5
II Samuel 7:16	Luke 1:32-33
Micah 4:10	Revelation 12:2
Micah 5:2	Matthew 2:6
Micah 6:15	John 4:37
Micah 7:6	Luke 12:53
Micah 7:20	Luke 1:55

8

PAUL AND THE MESSAGE OF JESUS

Biblical Texts: II Corinthians 5:11-6:2; and Romans 8:18-39.

In II Corinthians 5:11-6:2 Paul talks about the importance of the work of Christ and the present implications of that work.
In Romans 8:18-39 Paul discusses the Christian's future victory.

The Apostle Paul is the largest single contributor to the content of the New Testament. He wrote 13 epistles, and a large portion of the book of Acts is about his ministry. Paul's teaching regarding the work of Christ is a major key in understanding Christ's work.

As we noted in chapters three through six of this book, while we were studying the message of Christ, the total significance of Christ is not only in his message but also in what he did. Since Christ ascended into heaven shortly after the crucifixion-resurrection-ascension events, we do not find a lot of teaching coming from Christ himself about the significance of his acts. The bulk of the writings of Paul, however, is a commentary on the significance of what Christ did.

Paul and the Message of Jesus

As we have seen in previous chapters, the message of Jesus is the message about Jesus. We have summed up Jesus' message as:

> 1. The kingdom has come,
> 2. The kingdom is coming, and
> 3. I am the way.

Jesus' message about himself is that he is the one who ushers in the kingdom. This kingdom was the expectation of Israel. Jesus taught that this kingdom has arrived in certain aspects and in other aspects it was still coming.

Paul has virtually nothing to say about the kingdom. This might at first lead one to believe that the messages of Paul and Jesus were quite different. But in actuality their messages are very similar. Paul has Christ as the central theme of his message. He speaks about the present effects of Christ's ministry, and he talks about the ongoing effects of Christ's ministry.

The Centrality of Christ

Both Paul and Jesus taught that the person and work of Jesus is the primary point in their messages. Paul told the Corinthians, "I resolved to know nothing while I was with you except Jesus Christ and him crucified (I Corinthians 2:2 NIV)." Paul agreed with Jesus in seeing Jesus as the way to gain access to God the Father. He referred to Christ as the "power and wisdom of God (I Corinthians 1:24)."

Paul also agreed with Jesus in seeing that all the Old Testament Scriptures foretold the coming of Christ, and that Jesus fulfilled those prophecies. In Acts 26:19–23 we read Paul's words to King Agrippa explaining his ministry. Paul says, "I am saying nothing beyond what the prophets and Moses said would happen—that the Christ would suffer and, as the first to rise from the dead, would proclaim light to his own people and to the Gentiles (22-23 NIV)."

In II Corinthians 5:14–15 Paul explains the significance of Christ's death for us: "For Christ's love compels us, because we are convinced that one died for all, and therefore all died. And he died for all that those who live should no longer live for themselves, but for him who died for them and was raised again (NIV)."

Resurrection! I Cor. 15:20-22; Col. 1:1F; II Cor. 4:14 But, past res. of believer! Eph. 2:5,6; Ro. 6:4,5 So, res. of inner man is part 2 — res. of outer man still future. I Cor. 15:45! - successive reign of two comprehensive principles (kingdoms?), each with an Adam of its own! When did Xt become life-giving Spirit? cf. v. 22

The Present Effects of Christ's Ministry

While we noted that Paul has virtually nothing to say about the kingdom, he has much to say about the coming of Christ and the effect it has had. In chapter two we saw that Judaism in the time of Christ had an expectation of a future age. This was not always described as a coming kingdom. Paul does not describe the coming of the kingdom as John and Jesus did, but he does see that the expected future age has come with Jesus Christ. There are many passages of Scripture which might be used to point out this theme in Paul, but two will suffice.

In Galatians 4:4-5, Paul says, "When time had fully come, God sent his Son, born of a woman, born under law, to redeem those under law, that we might receive the full rights of sons (NIV)." For Paul "the time" had come. It had come in a sense which it had never come before, it had "fully come." In this description, we may see that Paul saw the coming of Christ as ushering in a new time—a new age. This new age can be correlated to the arrival of the kingdom of heaven for it too came with the arrival of Jesus Christ.

We previously observed how Jesus is central to the message of Paul. In doing this we looked at II Corinthians 5:14 and 15. Paul follows his statement on the significance of Christ's death with a statement on the present effect of the work of Christ. "Therefore, if anyone is in Christ, he is a new creation; the old has gone, the new has come (NIV)!" The tense of the verb is present: "Is a new creation." Paul is saying that because of the work of Christ, those who are his people are fundamentally different. They are a new creation. Paul describes this new creation as a state of being reconciled with God (5:18).

In II Corinthians 6:2, Paul quotes Isaiah 49:8, "In the time of my favor I heard you, and in the day of salvation I helped you (NIV)." He then adds his own commentary, "I tell you, now is the time of God's favor, now is the day of salvation (NIV)." Here again Paul sees the time brought in by Jesus Christ as the eschatological day of salvation.

Paul's reference to the fullness of time and the day of salvation show an agreement with the arrival of the kingdom of heaven as taught by John the Baptist and Jesus, but the reference to the day of salvation also has an ongoing character to it. Paul deals with the ongoing character of the work of Christ at more length in the epistle to the Romans 8:18-39.

The Future Effects of Christ's Ministry

The ongoing character of Christ's work has two effects according to the letters of Paul. These are: (1) for the moment we suffer, and (2) in the future we will be victorious.

a. We suffer because there is an ongoing struggle with sin. This takes place within ourselves as Paul explained in chapter seven of Romans. Paul says: "But I see another law at work in the members of my body, waging war against the law of my mind and making me a prisoner of the law of sin at work within my members (7:23 NIV)."

b. This struggle, however, is not only within ourselves, but it is also a struggle with forces without, as Paul says in Ephesians 6:12. "For our struggle is not against flesh and blood, but against the rulers, against the authorities, against the power of this dark world and against the spiritual forces of evil in the heavenly realms (NIV)."

Despite these struggles, Paul says that we may be very optimistic, because the outcome is clear. "No, in all these things we are more than conquerors through him who loved us. For I am convinced that neither death or life, neither angels nor demons, neither the present nor the future, nor any powers, neither height nor depth, nor anything else in all creation, will be able to separate us from the love of God that is in Christ Jesus our Lord (Romans 8:37-39 NIV)."

Summary

We may summarize the message of Paul and Jesus with a brief comparison of their messages:

Jesus	Paul
1. The kingdom has come	1. Now is the day of salvation
2. The kingdom is coming	2. We are more than conquerors
3. I am the way	3. Christ is the power and wisdom of God

Questions for Review

1. In what way is Christ central to the message of Paul?

2. Compare and contrast the message of Paul with the message of Jesus. *contrast: more emph. of sign. of acts — no specific kingdom teaching — compare: already/not yet — xt the center*

3. According to Paul what are the present effects of Christ's ministry? *Believers share in res. life*

4. According to Paul what are the future effects of Christ's ministry? *victory; sanct.; resurr.*

Questions for Discussion

1. Why do you suppose Paul uses the term "fullness of time" rather than "kingdom of heaven"? *Stressing new age / Xt.*

2. Paul stands historically opposite John the Baptist—one before and one after Jesus. Can you relate the messages of John and Paul to each other? *Here He comes! / That's what He did!*

3. Why do you suppose God allowed one man, Paul, to be so significant in the early church? *READ Bruce*

4. Compare Paul, a preeminent New Testament figure, with Moses, the preeminent Old Testament figure. *Prophet!*

9

PAUL AND JUDAISM

Biblical Texts: Ephesians 1:1-14; Romans 3 and 4.

In Ephesians 1:1-14 Paul gives us a doxology—a hymn of praise—to the Triune God for his work in salvation. Paul gives the role of each member of the Trinity in the securing of our salvation.

In Romans 3 and 4, Paul is discussing the status of Jews and Gentiles alike as they stand in terms of God's favor.

In the previous chapter, we considered how the message of Paul related to the message of Jesus. Now we need to tie Paul's message in with the matters we dealt with in the first and second chapters, namely the cultural and religious situation of the first century A.D.

Paul's place in the religious and cultural world of the first century A.D. was similar to that of John the Baptist and Jesus in that all were Jewish and shared the same ethnic background and religion. As was pointed out previously, however, Judaism of the first century was not nearly as homogeneous as Judaism is today. There were many differences among the Jews of Paul's day. Paul came from a Jewish background which was quite different from that of John and Jesus. We know something of Paul's life from his epistles.

It appears that Paul came from an upper middle class Jewish family. His home, unlike Jesus, was not in Palestine, the Jewish homeland, but rather was in what is present day Turkey. Paul had a strong religious education under one of the foremost scholars of the day, and again unlike Jesus was of the Pharasaic strain of Judaism. Much of what Paul says may be seen as directed towards Jewish beliefs of that day. We know that in his journey Paul always took his message to the Jews first. It is helpful to analyze some of the beliefs of the Jews at Paul's time in order to better understand Paul.

Because the letters of Paul were in prominent use during the Protestant Reformation to argue that salvation came by faith and not by works, many people view this to be the basic message of Paul. It is also sometimes thought that the message, "We are saved by faith and not by works," means that the Jewish people of Paul's day believed that they could be saved by works. Such is simply not the case. Paul's message is one of salvation by faith, but it is not the case that the Jewish religion believed in salvation by works.

Judaism as a religion can perhaps never be truly understood by anyone who is not Jewish. But we can make a reasonable effort to understand the beliefs of the Jews. The greatest mistake made by Gentile Christians regarding Judaism stems from the fact that Christianity is primarily a religion of salvation. Gentile Christians, therefore, often try and understand Judaism in terms of its doctrine of salvation. Judaism, however, is not a religion that is preoccupied with salvation as is Christianity. It is not now, and was not in Paul's day primarily concerned with the question: What must I do to be saved? It is very difficult for Christians to understand this, but if they want to truly understand Judaism they must try.

If Judaism is not concerned with salvation, what then is it concerned with? If we try to understand it and explain it in the fairest way possible, we would have to say the primary concern of Judaism is: How does one live a holy life? This was certainly the case in the times of Jesus and Paul. In the pages of the New Testament itself, we see Jesus and Paul criticizing the Jews and often assume that Judaism was generally "off the track." In all fairness we would have to admit, that while the Pharisees do become the subject of criticism, both Jesus and Paul have a basic respect for them.

Jesus recognized the Pharisees as models of righteousness (Matthew 5:20). Paul sees great advantage in his having been Jewish

↳ "Unless your righteousness surpasses that..."

(Romans 3:1–2). We must recognize that if we base our analysis of Judaism only on the criticism of Jesus and Paul, we have only part of the picture for Jesus and Paul were themselves Jewish! Being Jews they endorsed by their lives much that was positive about the Jewish faith.

What is very clear in the New Testament is that the Pharisees had a strong concern for purity and obedience of the law. They are very much occupied with maintaining holiness. It appears that the need for salvation was not a primary concern of Jews in the first century. Why were they not concerned, as Christians are today, with salvation? Let us see why.

In the second chapter of this book, we discussed Rabbinic Judaism and the *Talmud*. There is a section in the *Talmud* which expresses the Jewish view of salvation: "All Israel has a part in the world to come. It is written: 'Then will all your people be righteous . . . (Isaiah 60:21).'" (Sanhedrin 10:1, author's translation.) The *Talmud* then goes on to discuss various people who do not have a place in the world to come because of something that was written about them in the Scriptures. The basic view is that all Israel will be saved unless someone was so bad that the Bible explicitly states that they were damned.

It is specifically against this view that we find the apostle Paul writing. His view is that one's place in the world to come is not assured by being an Israelite but is rather assured by being one of God's chosen people. For Paul, God's chosen people are not the biological descendants of Abraham, but rather those who God has chosen according to his foreknowledge. We see Paul's position explained and defended in Romans 3 and 4, but we also see it systematically presented in Ephesians 1:1–14.

The Work of The Triune God in Salvation

Paul begins his letter to the Ephesians with a doxology in praise of the Triune God and specifically enumerates the work of each member of the Trinity in the salvation of the believer. With respect to the Father, Paul says:

> Praise be to the God and Father of our Lord Jesus Christ, who has blessed us in the heavenly realms with every spiritual blessing in Christ. For he chose us in him before the creation of the world to be holy and blameless in his sight. In love he predestined us to be adopted as his sons through Jesus Christ, in accordance with his pleasure and will—to the praise of his glorious grace which he has freely given us in the One he loves.
>
> Ephesians 1:3-6 NIV

In these verses, Paul attributes to <u>the Father the role of electing the believer</u>. The meaning and implications of election are largely overlooked by evangelical Christians today. The emphasis is rather on conversion. In the Scriptures, however, the emphasis is clearly the other way around. The words "conversion" and "convert" occur a total of twelve times in the whole Bible; the words "election" and "elect" occur 27 times (Authorized Version). Even more serious than the lack of emphasis on the biblical doctrine of election among evangelicals today is the widespread misunderstanding of it. <u>It is largely conceived of as a choosing of people who have chosen Christ.</u> An example of this is found in H. A. Ironsides' commentary of this passage in which he explains:

> When asked to explain the doctrine of election a colored brother once said, "Well, it's this way, the Lord done voted for my salvation; the devil done voted for my damnation; and I done voted with the Lord, and so we got into the majority."

This picture is inconsistent with the biblical picture of the sovereignty of God, in which his almighty power is never described as limited in any way by man's will. If divine election is to be compared to human vote taking, then there must be only one vote counted —God's.

The significance of the believer's election of God is to be found in the statement of the Apostle Paul in Ephesians 2:9, "No one can boast." Human pride is unconditionally excluded from the regenerate life.

Paul continues his doxology:

> In him [Christ] we have redemption through his blood, the forgiveness of sins, in accordance with the riches of God's grace that he lavished on us with all wisdom and understanding.
> Ephesians 1:-8, NIV

The role of Christ in the salvation of individuals is specifically stated by the apostle as that of redemption. This redemption is accomplished through the blood of Christ. Since the Middle Ages, theologians have discussed the question, "Why was it necessary for Christ to die?" Modern day liberal theologians do not consider the death of Christ as having been a necessity. They see the death of Jesus as an example for us. This attitude is a rejection of Paul's statement that, "We have redemption through his blood." The question, "Why was it necessary for Christ to die" is still a valid question for the one who accepts Paul's statements as revelation, for the question relates to man's need of redemption: "Why was it necessary to redeem mankind?"

The answer to this question is to be found in the teaching of Scripture that sin bears a penalty. From the outset, this has been included in divine revelation as a warning. "But you must not eat of the tree of the knowledge of good and evil, for when you eat of it you will surely die (Genesis 2:17, NIV)." That sin bears a penalty is included in revelation to Noah (Genesis 9:6) and Moses (Leviticus 20:2, 9, 10). It was given in revelation from Christ (Matthew 5:21-22), and in revelation which came through Paul, "For the wages of sin is death (Romans 6:23 NIV)."

The penalty for sin expresses God's wrath against sin, as Paul says of God's wrath, it is revealed from heaven against all ungodliness and unrighteousness of men (Romans 1:18). But, this God of wrath is also described in Scripture with the phrase, "God is love (I John 4:8)." God's wrath and love is expressed in Paul's illustration of the potter in Romans 9 who is making some pots for common use and some for good use. These pots for good use, however, are also sinners. They are vessels for good use only because, "God made him who had no sin to be sin for us, so that in him we might become the righteousness of God (II Corinthians 5:21, NIV)." The redemption of the elect is the role of the Son. He bears the penalty for sin on their behalf so that they might pass from condemnation to justification.

The doctrine of the Trinity, which many say is not explicit in the Scriptures, is affirmed by Paul as he describes what happens when one believes.

> In Him [Christ], you also, after listening to the message of truth, the gospel of your salvation—having also believed, you were sealed in Him with the Holy Spirit of promise, who is given as a pledge of our inheritance, with a view to the redemption of God's own possession, to the praise of His glory.
> Ephesians 1:13–14, *The New American Standard Bible*, copyright: The Lockman Foundation

3. The work of the Holy Spirit in the salvation of men is that of sealing the believer. The term "sealing" is not one that is normally listed as one of the steps in salvation. Nevertheless, it is a biblical term to describe the work of the third person of the Trinity. The Greek word translated here has a range of meaning very similar to the English word with which it is translated. The words equally refer to authentication and preservation. Just as a seal on a doctor's or lawyer's license authenticates it, so the Holy Spirit outwardly authenticates the believer. Christ says that "Every good tree brings forth good fruit (Matthew 7:17 NIV)." And again, "A tree is recognized by its fruit (Matthew 12:33 NIV)." Galatians 5:22 tells us that it is the Spirit which produces fruit in the life of the believer authenticating him—making him recognizable as a believer. The other meaning of "seal", that of preservation, as when we speak of the seal on a jar, is not elsewhere explicitly identified as a work of the Spirit. But, the preservation of the believer is known from Christ's word in John 10:28, "No one can snatch them out of my hand." Thus Paul explains the double function of the work of the Spirit as authentication and preservation.

We may summarize the work of the Trinity in the salvation of men as follows: the Father elects, the Son redeems, and the Spirit sanctifies. The apostle Paul is saying that those whom the Father elects, are redeemed by the Son, and sanctified by the Spirit, are the ones who have a place in the world to come.

Questions for Review

1. What is the major concern of Judaism?

2. Why is Paul concerned that his readers understand the doctrine of election?

3. What is the role of the various members of the Trinity in salvation?

4. Are Jews and Gentiles separate peoples of God today?

Questions for Discussion

1. Do you agree with the author's appraisal of the main concern of Judaism? Why?

2. Is what Paul said about Jews and their place in the world to come still valid for Jews today?

3. Why do you think that Jews in Paul's time believed that all Israel had a place in the world to come?

4. Do the things considered in this chapter have any bearing on evangelism of the Jews today?

10

THE NECESSITY OF CHRIST

Biblical Text: Hebrews 1 and 2

The first two chapters of Hebrews are primarily about the superiority of Christ over angels.

As we mentioned in the second chapter, Judaism was far more diverse in character during the first century than is the case today. The Jews were expecting a Messiah, but ideas about him differed. Several people had appeared who claimed to be the Messiah. All, however, failed in their messianic mission. As we see in the gospels, it appears that for a short time after his death, the disciples thought that Jesus had failed as a Messiah and had proved himself to be an impostor. But the true character of Christ's ministry was not realized until after the resurrection. While we read of many converts in the early church, most of the Jews were not convinced that Jesus was the Christ—the Messiah. They continued to look for one who would fulfill their expectations.

One of the things that had particularly irked the Jews for years was foreign dominance of their land. They had been subject to the overlordship of one ruler or another for almost all of the time that had passed since the conquest of Jerusalem in 586 B.C. In 66 A.D. a rebellion was organized against the Roman rulers, and perhaps much to everyone's surprise it succeeded! The Roman yoke was thrown off. Israel became a sovereign nation once more. Today we know how short lived that rebellion was, but in 68 A.D. it looked to the Jews as if the end of times had at last come—the kingship was again restored to Israel. Jerusalem was no more trodden underfoot by the nations. Sacrifices of thanks went up from the temple daily.

Hebrew Christians 68 A. D.

This turn of affairs must have made serious problems for the Hebrew Christians in Jerusalem. Remember how, for many of them, accepting Jesus as the Messiah did not come easily. Perhaps many of them had originally been looking forward to a militant Messiah who would establish an earthly kingdom ushering in a new and wonderful age for the Jews. When Jesus came he said such things as "my kingdom is not of this world," "I go to prepare a place for you," etc. Gradually they readjusted their thinking to expect the sort of kingdom of which Jesus taught. They came to believe in a kingdom which had a present and a future aspect—a kingdom that brought salvation now but the fullness of which was still future.

In 66 A.D. when the Jews were successful in throwing off the Roman overlordship, it must have looked to some like the great day they had expected. Perhaps some Hebrew Christians were given to second thoughts about Jesus. Maybe they were beginning to think that those Jews who had not been convinced by Jesus were right. Maybe they were thinking of returning to Judaism as they had known it before they became followers of Jesus. Perhaps they wanted to keep some of the traditional elements of Judaism and still be followers of Jesus. Whatever the case, it is plain that the period of the success of the Jewish rebellion was a difficult time for the Hebrew Christians in Jerusalem.

Hebrew Christians in 66 A.D.

Judaism	*Christianity*
* Present	* Scattered
* Militant	* Persecuted
* Victorious	* Outcast
* Successful	* Successful

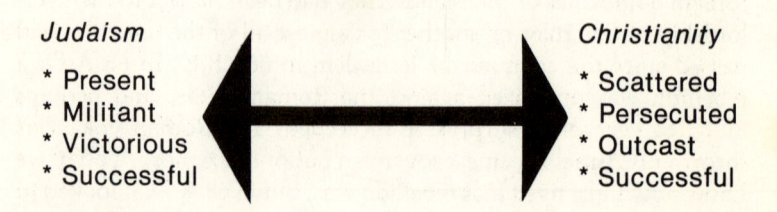

Roman XII legion moves to quell the rebellion

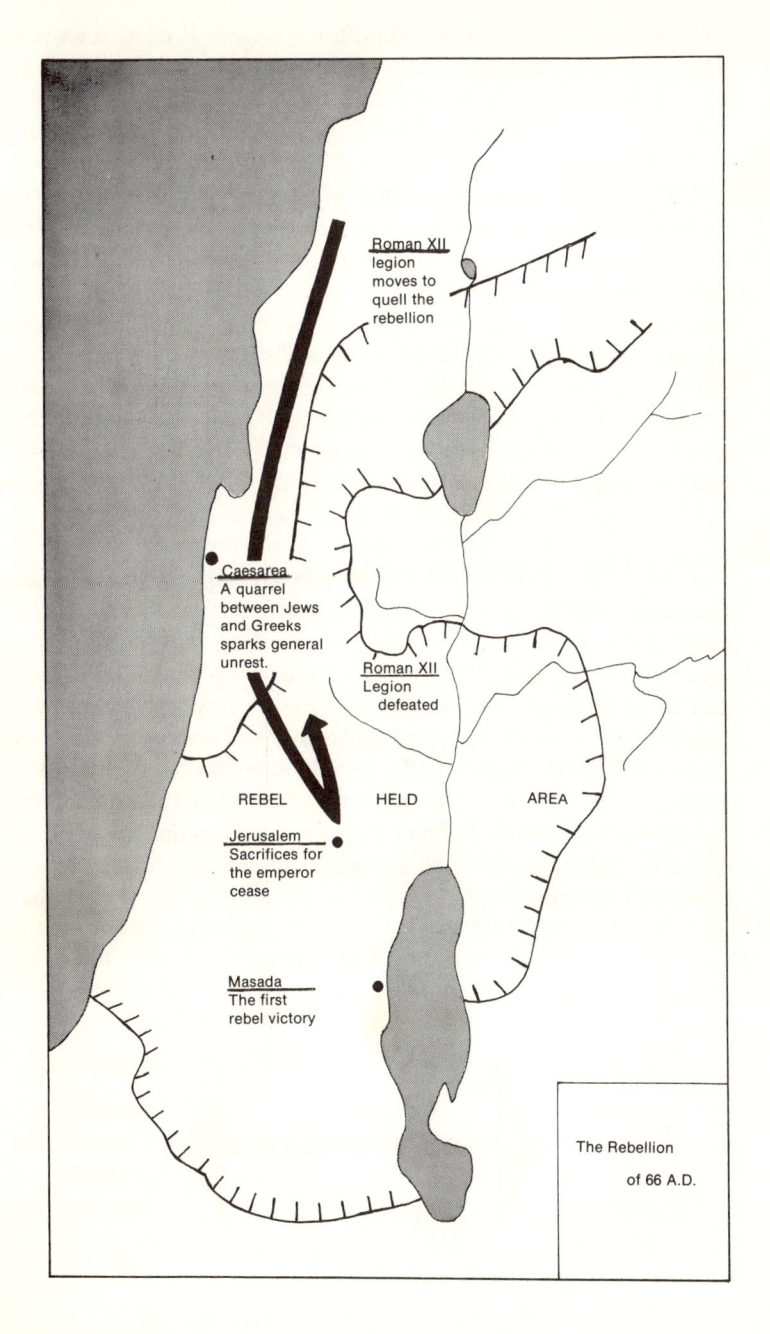

Caesarea
A quarrel between Jews and Greeks sparks general unrest.

Roman XII Legion defeated

REBEL HELD AREA

Jerusalem
Sacrifices for the emperor cease

Masada
The first rebel victory

The Rebellion of 66 A.D.

There are reasons to believe that the epistle to the Hebrews was written to the Hebrew Christians in Jerusalem during this time. There are indications that the people to whom it was written were tempted with apostasy (10:23). They were living in a time when the sacrifices were still being performed (10:1). Many of the customs and practices of the Jews were discussed. Most important of all, the epistle to the Hebrews presents a very strong message that was needed in just such a time: In contrast with other heavenly and earthly beings, Christ provides salvation.

The Person of Jesus Christ

In chapters 1–5, the author begins to build his argument for the superiority of Christ. He shows that the incarnation makes Christ's high priesthood superior to the earthly high priesthood.

The author does not begin to deal with the incarnation directly, but rather begins with Christ's sonship. He shows that two aspects of this sonship are Christ's divine and human natures. The divine nature is demonstrated in Christ's being, "the radiance of God's glory and the exact representation of his being (1:3 NIV)." The human nature of Christ is demonstrated in the brotherhood of Christ to mankind. For this reason he had to be made like his brothers in every way, in order that he might become a merciful and faithful high priest in service to God, and that he might make atonement for the sins of the people (2:17 NIV)."

These initial arguments, that in the son we have the divine and human natures, are used to show Christ's superiority over the angels (whom the Essenes viewed as having a messianic work), and over Moses (the preeminent personality of the religion of the Hebrews). Christ, superior over all the creatures heavenly and earthly, is the basis of the exhortation to hold fast to Christianity.

The Divine Nature of Christ

Before dealing with the divine nature of Christ, the author first affirms Christ's divinity as the radiance of God's glory and the stamp of his being. This explanation of Christ's divine nature is based in

88

part on portions of the Old Testament which related directly to the line of David. The author does not explain how he derived that these passages are in some sense related to the Messiah, but we have seen in previous chapters of this book that such ideas were prevalent in Israel at this time.

Due to this prevalent view, our author can express the opinion that the promise to David in II Samuel 7 is applicable to the Messiah, affirming his special relationship to the father which the angels do not share: "I will be his father, and he will be my son. When he does wrong I will punish him with the rod of men, with floggings inflicted by men (NIV)."

The important conclusion to which our author points is that in the divine nature of Christ one may recognize (1) the eternal nature, (2) the just nature, and (3) the exalted nature of Christ. These are brought out by the selection of quotations from Psalms 45 and 102.

(1) The eternal nature is shown by the quotations,
Your throne, O God, will last for ever and ever (Hebrews 1:8 NIV). and,
Like a garment they will be changed.
But you remain the same,
and your years will never end (Hebrews 1:12 NIV).
and the portion of Psalm 102 which follows but did not need to be quoted,
The children of your servants will live in your
presense; their descendants will be established before you (Psalm 102:28 NIV).

(2) The just nature of Christ is brought out in the quotation of Psalm 45, "You have loved righteousness and hated wickedness (Hebrews 1:9 NIV)."

(3) The exalted nature of Christ is presented first by a quotation from Deuteronomy 32:43, "Let all God's angels worship him (Hebrews 1:6 NIV)."[1] In citing this as a reference to the Messiah, one might be baffled if not aware of the context. The ending of Deuteronomy 32 is in praise of the final triumph of God. This

triumph was exclusively conceived as a messianic triumph in the Hebrew religion of the pre-Christian and early-Christian eras. In this framework, the passage is of nessessity messianic.

The exalted nature of Christ is further supported by Psalm 45:7, "your God has set you above your companions, by anointing you with the oil of joy (Hebrews 1:8 NIV);" and by Psalm 110:1, "Sit at my right hand until I make your enemies a footstool for your feet (Hebrews 1:13 NIV)."

This son then, begotten of the Father (1:5 quoting Psalm 2:7) is eternal, just, and exalted. This nature is superior to the angels who, although heavenly beings, are nevertheless created servants as supported by the quotation of Psalm 104:4, "He makes his angels winds, his servants flames of fire (Hebrews 1:7 NIV)."

Having in this manner clearly established the facts and implications of the divine nature, our author turns to the facts and implications of the human nature of his divine son.

Human Nature of Christ

The first fact of the humanity of Christ which our author explains is this: In being human, Christ is not inferior, but rather superior to the angels. This is established by reiterating that God's purpose for man is dominion. Man is but for a short while, lower than the angels.[2] This is supported by a quotation from Psalm 8:5-7,

You made him for a little while lower than the angels;
 you crowned him with glory and honor
 and put everything under his feet.
                                    Hebrews 2:7-8 NIV footnote

The message of this Psalm is that God has been gracious to man in creation. In creation, God has set up man as the master. This is an echo of the statement in Genesis 1:28,

Be fruitful and increase in number; fill the earth and subdue it. Rule over the fish of the sea and the birds of the air and over every living creature that moves on the ground.

NIV

This dominion is not a present but rather an eschatological or future fact. It must, therefore, be accomplished messianically, and in our author's explanation, it is accomplished through the incarnation. His reasoning is something like this:

(Fact 1) Christ is:
  (A) Human, and through suffering is   (Heb. 2:9)
  (B) crowned with glory and honor.
(Therefore) Man is:
  (A) Human, and through identification with Christ's suffer-will be
  (B) crowned with glory and honor.[3]   (Heb. 2:10)

This incarnation is God's way of reestablishing his original purpose in creation. It is as the author says "fitting" for "Both the one who makes men holy and those who are made holy are of the same family (Hebrews 2:11 NIV)". In "bringing many sons to glory" (cf. v. 10) Christ is a consecrating priest. Furthermore, this explains the Old Testament references in Psalm 22:22,

I will declare your name to my brothers;
  in the presence of the congregation I will sing
    your praises.

Hebrews 2:12 NIV

and Isaiah 8:18,
  Here am I, and the children God has given me

Hebrews 2:13 NIV

The messianic character of Psalm 22 was clearly established in the mind of the early church by Christ's use of its opening sentence while on the cross. And the messianic prophecy of Isaiah's work was seen in statements about himself being typological. Because of this sort of understanding of the Old Testament, our author argued that there was to be a brotherhood of the Messiah and the elect. In seeing that the Old Testament also taught that all things were to be placed in subjection to man; then, Christ as man is superior to the angels. He has already attained the eschatological goal of glory and honor.

Conclusion

The point at which the author is getting is simply this: <u>Now that we have Jesus Christ, we have something greater than anyone had under the Old Testament religion.</u> As we have briefly mentioned and as we will see in the next chapter, the possession of a better faith is the basis of an exhortation to the Hebrew Christians not to turn back to their old religion.

[1] This passage does not appear in most English Bibles. It appears in the Septuagint version and in 4QDeut^q from Qumran. The Septuagint and Qumran versions of Deuteronomy are not identical but are similar. This one line, however, appears in both. In the view of recent textual theories which have risen since the Qumran discoveries, the combined support argue for the authenticity of this reading. Recent textual theories have been outlined in F.M. Cross and S. Talmon, *Qumran and the History of the Biblical Text* (1975).

[2] The Greek and Hebrew here may be taken as either "less" in time or in position. The theological context allows either except when construed eschatologically, and then it must be seen as meaning a brief time.

[3] This is the same sort of reasoning Paul uses in I Corinthians 15:20-28

Questions for Review

1. What is the major theme of the epistle to the Hebrews?

2. Why does the author of Hebrews bother to point out that Christ is superior to angels?

3. Compare and contrast Judaism and Christianity in 6*6* A.D.

4. What messianic Psalms are quoted in the epistle to the Hebrews, chapters 1 and 2? *2, 104, 45, 102, 110, 8, 22*

5. What is the significance of the divine nature of Christ? The human nature of Christ? *eternal, just, exalted*   *Man glorified*

Questions for Discussion

1. This chapter discussed the Hebrew Christian's probable feelings in 66 A.D. How do you think Gentile Christians generally viewed the events of 66 A.D.?

2. Having studied the apostles and Paul in the previous chapters, do you think that Paul wrote the epistle to the Hebrews?

3. Study the way the writer of Hebrews uses the Old Testament and compare or contrast his use of the Old Testament with that of the apostles as discussed in chapter seven of this textbook.

4. Do you agree with the position presented in this book regarding the date and addressees of Hebrews? If not, does this affect the interpretation?

11

THE SHADOW AND THE REALITY

Biblical Text: Hebrews 8–9

In chapters 8 and 9 of Hebrews, the author discusses how Christ is the reality of those things which were anticipated under the Old Testament system of worship.

Before looking at what the author has to say in chapters eight and nine of Hebrews, we should briefly survey what he says in chapters three through seven. There he talks about the work of Christ in terms of Christ's superiority over the Old Testament system of worship.

The Work of Christ

The author of the epistle of Hebrews describes the work of Christ under three basic headings: 1) The high priesthood of Christ, 2) The temptation of Christ, and 3) The resurrection of Christ.

The High Priesthood of Christ

The author was previously speaking about the incarnation of Christ and makes his transition to the high priesthood, by showing that the incarnation was necessary for Christ to be a high priest. This fact is bound up in the very definition of a high priest.

> Every high priest is selected from among men and is appointed to represent them in matters related to God, to offer gifts and sacrifices for sins.
>
> Hebrews 5:1 NIV

Christ fulfilled the role of a high priest once and for all. This is reason to reprove those who were tempted to look for a future messianic priest or those who were tempted to put faith in the contemporary high priestly sacrifices.

The incarnation was necessary for three aspects of the priesthood. It was necessary for Christ to be (1) one who consecrates, (2) to be merciful and faithful, and (3) to offer up sacrifices.

(1) Christ's bringing many sons to glory is identified in 2:10–11 as a consecrating function. It is therefore necessary that he be human for, "... the one who makes men holy and those who are made holy are of the same family (2:11 NIV)."

(2) The incarnation was necessary in order for him to be merciful and faithful. This mercy and faithfulness is explained in 2:18 as a result of the test of suffering. Having experienced these himself he is able to help those who are currently going through these tests.

(3) Finally, the incarnation was necessary for Christ to offer up a sacrifice for sin. Since angels do not sacrifice and it would also be preposterous for God to offer up sacrifices to himself, Christ therefore became man that he might be appointed from among men to be their representative in offering up a sacrifice (5:1).

The Temptation of Christ

Given what has already been said about the situation of our readers, it is not surprising to find that at this point the author jumps to a long digression of which the point is, "... let us hold firmly to the faith we profess (4:14 NIV)." The digression turns to Moses and the days of trial for Israel in the wilderness. The author is making a twofold analogy from this situation.

```
                          is compared to
The wilderness experience ───────────────▶ the reader's situation
                          │
                          │  is compared to
                          └───────────────▶ Christ's temptation
```

The Sons of Israel in the wilderness failed to realize God's mercy and did not enter into his rest. The exhortation to the readers, however, is to enter in. The difference in the present situation is that the readers have "timely help". Or as the author says, "Therefore, since we have a great high priest who has gone into heaven, Jesus the Son of God, let us hold firmly to the faith we profess. For we do not have a high priest who is unable to sympathize with our weaknesses . . . (4:14–15 NIV)." This may be found because he is, ". . . one who has been tempted in every way, just as we are—yet without sin (4:15 NIV)."

The temptation of Christ and his successful maintenance of holiness in the face of it demonstrates understanding of our situation which could not have happened apart from the incarnation.

The Resurrection of Christ

A further point which the author makes is that:

> Since the children have flesh and blood, he too shared in their humanity so that by his death he might destroy him who holds the power of death—that is the devil—and free those who all their lives were held in slavery by their fear of death. For surely it is not angels he helps, but Abraham's descendants.
> Hebrews 2:14–16 NIV

The author's point here is that the incarnation was necessary to overcome death. Christ had to be made human to experience death, as this was necessary to break the power of death. The crowning feat of Christ's work is to, "free those who all their lives were held in slavery by their fear of death (Hebrews 2:14 NIV)."

Summary

In the scheme of the author of the epistle to the Hebrews, the purposes and effects of the incarnation are wound together. Each purpose brought about an effect and each effect came from a divine purpose. The effects and purposes may be listed as follows:

1. To provide an eternal high priest, who once for all would offer a sacrifice for sin.

2. To provide a merciful and faithful high priest who would sympathize with our weaknesses, so that we might come boldly before the throne of God to receive mercy.

3. To reestablish God's original purpose for man in creation, to rule over all things with glory and honor.

4. To break the power of death and relieve mankind from the fear of death.

These are all conclusions which bolster the main objective of the letter, to exhort Christians to hold fast to their faith.

The Relationship of Hebrews to Paul and Jesus

Throughout the epistle to the Hebrews, the author uses words referring to the times and ages. In 1:1-2 he refers to these last days and to the past. In 2:5 he refers to the age to come. In 8:8-9 and following he refers to the old and new covenants. In 6:5 he speaks of the age to come. In 9:11 and 10:1 he speaks of the good things to come

In all of these references it is clear that he is distinguishing between two ages, as Paul did. (See chapter 9 of this book.)

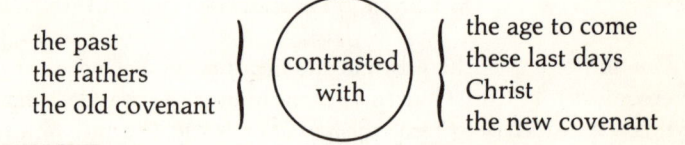

the past		the age to come
the fathers	contrasted with	these last days
the old covenant		Christ
		the new covenant

As we saw in the previous chapter, the present age is distinguished by Christ's having come: a fact which the readers seem to believe, but the author clearly reaffirms it. The coming of Christ has made a fundamental change in the worship of God. This fundamental change is Christ. The change is fundamental because of the person and the work of Jesus Christ. What then is the meaning of all that went before? What significance has the temple? The sacrifices? The priesthood?

To the Hebrew Christians in Jerusalem in 66-70 A.D., these questions were not merely academic. They were faced with the resurgence of Jewish power, a real temple, and ongoing sacrifices. To these people the answers to these questions affected the position they were to take in the worship of God.

The author of Hebrews seeks to answer these questions for the people to whom he is writing. He seeks to explain the difference by contrasting the Jewish perspective of history with what the Christian's perspective should be. The Jewish people had looked forward to a great eschatological age which would come. Our writer proclaims that the days in which they were then living were those last days. The writer says we are not looking forward to the age to come, but rather we are now looking forward to "All things in subjection (2:5-9)." In other words the age of expectation is over. The age of fulfillment has begun.

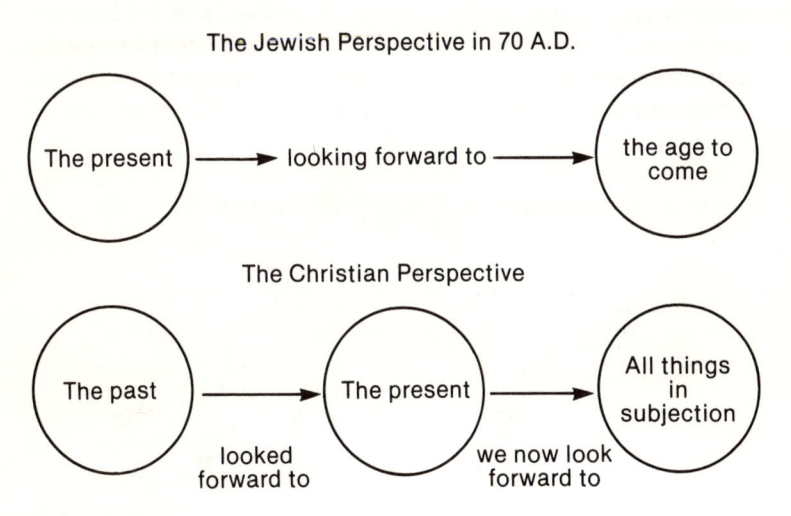

The Jewish Perspective in 70 A.D.

The present ⟶ looking forward to ⟶ the age to come

The Christian Perspective

The past ⟶ The present ⟶ All things in subjection
looked forward to | we now look forward to

Given this historical perspective, the writer understands that all Old Testament revelation is looking forward to what happened when Christ ushered in the age to come—the kingdom of heaven —the present age. It is for this reason the writer refers to the things of the Old Testament revelation as a shadow and a copy (8:5). They were revelatory in character and not the substance of the reality.

They were to teach about the heavenly reality which is now revealed in Christ.

("heavenly things" (9:23))

It is necessary here to consider for a while what is meant by heavenly reality. Often when we think of heavenly reality, we think of the way things are in heaven where God is. This is not exactly the meaning of our writer. "Heavenly" in the New Testament can mean essentially the same as what we often mean when we say spiritual. When we speak of the spiritual reality or spiritual things, we mean things that are present and very much with us but things which are transcendent and not tangible. We see the word "heavenly" takes on this meaning particularly in Ephesians when Paul speaks of having been blessed in heavenly places. Here he does not mean being blessed in the physical location known as heaven, but rather being blessed with spiritual blessings (Ephesians 1:3).

So too the author of Hebrews, when he speaks of the heavenly reality, does not necessarily mean the way things are in heaven. He sometimes is speaking of spiritual realities. It is in this sense that the writer says that the temple was a shadow of the heavenly reality. It was a picture of the spiritual truth.

The writer's view may be illustrated for simplicity:

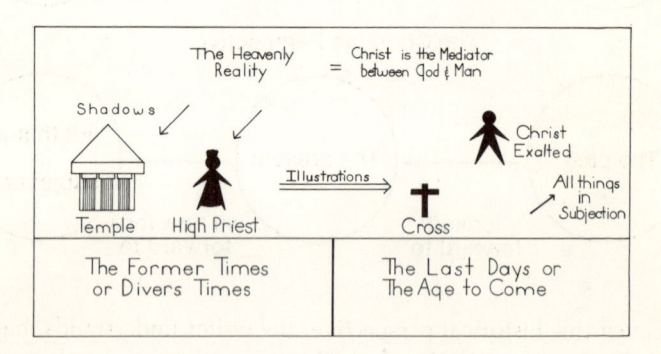

[Diagram: The Heavenly Reality = Christ is the Mediator between God & Man. Shadows: Temple, High Priest → Illustrations → Cross, Christ Exalted, All things in Subjection. The Former Times or Divers Times | The Last Days or The Age to Come]

We, like the writer of Hebrews, live in the "Age to Come." We look forward to all things in subjection to Christ. We cannot return to the conditions and situation of the former times. We cannot look for an earthly temple and high priest.

Questions for Review

1. Summarize the message of the author of Hebrews through chapter 9.

2. What are three basic headings under which the author of Hebrews discusses the work of Christ?

3. What are the purposes and effects of the incarnation?

4. What does the author of Hebrews mean by the "heavenly reality"?

Questions for Discussion

1. Hebrews is the only book in the New Testament which discusses the priesthood of Christ. Why do you think this is?

2. Compare the messages of Jesus, Paul, and the author of Hebrews.

3. Throughout the history of the church, theologians have continually discussed the question: Why was there an incarnation? Do you think you can answer this question?

4. Another question theologians have struggled with is: Why did Christ die? Can you answer this question?

12

THE COVENANT AND THE DISPENSATION

Biblical Texts: Jeremiah 31:31-40; Hebrews 8

> *Jeremiah 31:31-40 contains the prophecies of Jeremiah concerning a future age in which Israel would be restored and God would make a new covenant with them.*
>
> *Hebrews 8 contains the description of how Jesus is the high priest of a new covenant and quotes Jeremiah's prophecies as having been fulfilled in the New Testament era.*

Was the period in the Garden of Eden primarily a time of testing? Do Christians have a responsibility today to subdue the earth and rule over it?

If you answered the first question yes and the second no, it may be because you have been influenced by teachers who have been dispensational. If you answered the first no and the second yes, it may be because you have been influenced by teachers who take a covenantal position. If you answered both yes or no, you may have not been consistently influenced by either position. But the point is maybe you have taken a position and do not realize it.

The possible systems of presenting the overall message of the Bible are theoretically limitless, but in reality there are two systems used almost exclusively. Most theologians conscientiously choose one or the other of these systems to the exclusion of the other. Most mature Christian laymen have taken sides unwittingly with one or the other camps of theologians.

These two positions are <u>covenantal theology and dispensationalism</u>. Most laymen do not recognize either term as having any meaning for them, and would not profess to take either position. In reality most laymen take a position unwittingly by embracing the distinctive elements of one position and rejecting the beliefs of the other.

Unlike the laymen the theologians have quite consciously taken sides:

> It is the writer's conviction that the larger part of the futuristic dispensational scheme, though exciting, is errant, the errancy compounded by an inordinate desire for the knowledge of "things to come" with little desire for the knowledge of holiness.—George C. Miladin in *Is This Really The End?* (Cherry Hills, N.J.: Mack, 1972)

> The Word of Truth, then, has right divisions and it must be evident that, as one cannot be "a workman that needed not be ashamed" without observing them, so *any study* of the Word which ignores those divisions must be in large measure profitless and confusing.—C.I. Scofield in *Rightly Dividing The Word of Truth* (N.Y.: Bible Truth).

In view of the seriousness which these theologians attach to their views, and to what they view as the error of the opposite point of view, it is essential that every layman be aware that such positions exist. And it is important that the layman realize much of what he hears and reads is influenced by some of the basic ideas of these positions.

Dispensationalism

Beginning with dispensationalism, let us ask what these schools of thought are teaching. The origin of dispensationalism is usually attributed to John Nelson <u>Darby</u>, a leader of the <u>nineteenth-century Plymouth Brethren Movement</u>. In fact, certain elements of dispensationalist thought can be traced back to the early church.

Early Church Fathers, such as Augustine, spoke of dispensations. It seems to always have been recognized that there were different stages in God's dealing with mankind and these stages were often referred to as dispensations. But for the most part, the early church recognized two dispensations: The Old Testament or former dispensation and the New Testament or present dispensation.

J. N. Darby is truly the father of modern dispensationalism. For although there were others before him who spoke of more dispensations than two, and who saw important implications in their dispensational schemes, it was not until Darby that any sizable group of Christians saw dispensationalism as having practical implications and sought to promote it and apply it.

In more recent times dispensationalism found a most capable exponent in C. I. Scofield. He is responsible for the production of the *Scofield Chain Reference Bible* which brought a whole generation of Christians under dispensational teaching.

The effect of the *Scofield Chain Reference Bible* on the church is immeasurable. It may be credited with the promotion of Bible study among laymen. It provided him with a commentary on the Bible, with a theology, and with a sense of ability to handle the Scriptures for himself. It should be credited with promoting Calvinism among otherwise non-Calvinist churches. It may not have taught a lot of Calvinist doctrines, but it taught the assurance of salvation and eternal security—two facts which were contrary to positions of the Anabaptist and Arminian churches. Millions of copies of the *Scofield Bible* have been printed in the years since it was first produced. Since Scofield there has not been a single Bible teacher who has so profoundly influenced the church of Jesus Christ—whether it was for better or worse.

The dispensationalism of C. I. Scofield is the most representative of all dispensationalist thought, despite the fact that there are some points of disagreement among dispensationalist scholars.

C. I. Scofield describes his basic system in a small book entitled, *Rightly Dividing the Word of Truth*.

The Scriptures divided time (by which is meant the entire period from the creation of Adam to the "new heaven and a new earth" of Rev. 21:1) into seven unequal periods, usually called "Dispensations" (Eph. 3:2),

These periods are marked off in Scripture by some change in God's method of dealing with mankind, or a portion of mankind, with respect to two matters: sin, and man's responsibility. Each of the dispensations may be regarded as a new test of the natural man, and each ends in judgment—marking his utter failure in every dispensation.

Next Scofield describes the seven dispensations which are:

1. Man Innocent
2. Man under Conscience
3. Man in Authority over the Earth
4. Man under Promise
5. Man under Law
6. Man under Grace
7. Man under the Personal Reign of Christ.

Another important element of Scofield's system is found in a chapter entitled "The Jew, The Gentile, and the Church of God." Here he explains:

Whoever reads the Bible with any attention cannot fail to perceive that more than half of its contents relate to one nation—the Israelites. He perceives, too, that they have a very distinct place in the dealings and counsels of God. Separated from the mass of mankind, they are taken into covenant with Jehovah, who gives them specific promises not given to any other nation. Their history alone is told in Old Testament narrative and prophecy—other nations being mentioned only as they touch the Jew. It appears, also that all the communications of Jehovah to Israel as a nation relate to the Earth.

Continuing his researches, the student finds large mention in Scripture of another distinct body, which is called the Church. Instead of obedience bringing the reward of earthly greatness and wealth, the Church is taught to be content with food and raiment, and to expect persecution and hatred, and it is perceived that just as distinctly as Israel stands connected with temporal and earthly things, so distinctly does the Church stand connected with spiritual and heavenly things.

In the predictions concerning <u>the future of Israel and the Church the distinction is still more startling</u>. The Church will be taken away from the earth entirely, but restored Israel is yet to have her greatest earthly splendor and power.

These elements are perhaps the most distinctive elements of dispensationalism to the non-dispensationalist.

There is a modern dispensationalist who is currently beginning to rival Scofield in stature due to the publication of two extremely significant works. *The Ryrie Study Bible*[1] and *Dispensationalism Today*.[2] Charles Caldwell Ryrie cites what he believes to be <u>the essential elements of dispensationalism</u>—the *sine qua non*.

(1) A dispensationalist keeps Israel and the Church distinct.
(2) This distinction between Israel and the Church is born out of a system of hermeneutics which is usually called literal interpretation.
(3) To the dispensationalist the soteriological or saving program of God is not the only program but one of the means God is using in the total program of glorifying Himself.

Whatever the ramification of these points may be, we are safe in saying that they are a fair characterization of dispensationalism as a movement.

Covenant Theology

Covenant theology has never been explained quite so simply and clearly as dispensationalism has been. Covenant theologians have often been quite precise in their definitions but not necessarily intelligible to the layman. Covenant theologians have often been succinct and articulate. An excellent example is the statement of Cornelius Van Til in the *Twentieth Century Encyclopedia of Religious Knowledge*.

Covenant theology sprang up naturally as the most consistant expression of Calvinism, in which the idea of the self-sufficient ontological Trinity is the final reference point in all predication.[3]

Most people, including many with excellent educations, will have a difficulty understanding what is meant by, "the self-sufficient ontological Trinity." Van Til, however, knows exactly what is meant and has chosen his words very carefully so as to define his position with precision. It is not necessary, that covenant theology be defined with words which are not common place, but some accuracy will be lost in the simplification.

Covenant theology has, as Van Til explained, developed within a Calvinistic point of view. This does not mean that dispensationalists are strangers to Calvinism as many dispensationalists have been Calvinistic, nor does it mean that all Calvinists are covenantal theologians. The basic ideas of covenantal theology were present in the early church. But, it has been within the framework of Calvinism that it has found its fullest expression.

What, then, is covenant theology? Covenant theology is the belief that whatever comes to pass does so by the will of God. This includes: 1) the belief that God is sovereign in salvation, and 2) God has a singularity of purpose in dealing with mankind, and 3) God's dealing with mankind in this manner is reflected in the biblical covenants. While this definition does not clearly exhibit the differences between dispensationalism and covenantal theology, it highlights the beliefs that covenant theologians hold precious and feel are erroneously perceived by dispensationalists.

1) *Whatever comes to pass does so by the will of God*. Statements as to the sovereignty of God abound in the Scripture, and few Christians would deny God's sovereignty. The covenantal theologian, however, recognizes that the sovereignty of God is ultimate. God is sovereign in every way, over every thing—even evil.

Joseph, speaking to his brothers about the sin which they committed against him said: "You intended to harm me, but God intended it for good to accomplish what is now being done, the saving of many lives (Genesis 50:20 NIV)."

Joseph recognized that evil-minded men are subservient to God, and in doing evil they are ultimately serving God's sovereign will. In Joseph's case they caused much suffering, but ultimately they accomplished "what is now being done, the saving of many lives." Though they meant it for evil, God meant it for good.

2) *God has a singularity of purpose in dealing with mankind.* God is doing many things with mankind, but singularity of purpose is clear in the important points of history: creation, redemption, and fulfillment. At creation all mankind was given a singular purpose: "He blessed them and said to them, "Be fruitful and increase in number; fill the earth and subdue it (Genesis 1:28)." Salvation for all men is provided in a singular source, Jesus Christ: "For as in Adam all die, so in Christ all will be made alive (I Corinthians 15:22 NIV)." And when the end of time is reached all men are called to the judgment. God has not given the subduing of the earth to one group of men, nor salvation to men through various redeemers, nor will there be any consideration of the various breeds when he sorts the sheep and the goats.

3) *God's dealing with mankind is covenantal.* What is a covenant? The most frequently given answer is "an agreement between two or more people." There are covenants between two or more people found in the Bible, but covenant theologians of recent years, have seen this as an inadequate definition. Covenant as it applies to God's dealings with men is not correctly described as an agreement. It is rather *a sovereign promise of grace with stipulations.*

We see this covenantal character of God's dealing with men in God's covenant with Noah and in God's covenant with Abraham. (Genesis 9:8–17; 17:3–8). In these passages God establishes the covenant sovereignly. The covenants are God initiated, God defined, and do not require any agreement or acquiesence on man's part. The covenants are in character gracious. Noah is promised seed time and harvest, Abraham a land, a seed, and a blessing to the nations which would come through him. There are stipulations attached to these covenants. Noah is instructed regarding the manslayer; Abraham regarding circumcision.

The Covenant and the New Testament

The emphasis of covenant theology has clearly been the unity of God's working with men. To the covenant theologian there is no fundamental change in the way God deals with men in the Old Testament and New Testament times. The two testaments rather represent the difference between promise and fulfillment. The fundamental unity of the Old and New Testaments is seen in Jeremiah's prophecy of the new covenant.

The basic message of Jeremiah is that after punishment of Israel's sins God would restore Israel. It is a measure of blessing on Israel in this restoration that he will make a new covenant with Israel. What is new about the new covenant is not its content, but its internal character. It will be on the heart rather than on stone.

It is the message of Hebrews chapter 8 that this new covenant is established for Israel in Jesus. The old covenant is soon to pass away—that is, it was soon to pass away at the time the book of Hebrews was written (vs. 13). Those sacrifices have ceased as of 70 A.D. when the temple was destroyed. The old covenant has passed away.

The ministry of Jesus is superior to the mediator of the old covenant—the High Priest—as the covenant which he mediates is superior (vs. 6). The point is God is still dealing with men covenantally.

The Problem With Dispensationalism

Having stated the position of dispensationalism and the position of covenantal theology, what is at issue? Let us return to Ryrie's *sine qua non*, or essential elements of dispensationalism, which we may summarize as follows:

God has *different* economies in governing the world.
1. Israel and the church are different.
2. Interpret the Bible literally.
3. Salvation is *one* program God is using to glorify himself,

but it *not the only* program.

If this fairly characterizes dispensationalism, we could fairly specify the concerns of covenant theology as follows:

God has different economies in governing the world. This cannot mean that God changes his mind or has different plans of salvation for different segments of his people (James 1:17 and I Corinthians 15:22). What then is the purpose of this emphasis?

1. *Israel and the church are different*. With this the covenant theologian might agree, if he knew what "different" entailed. The people of Israel existed as a nation in the land of Israel before the church was established. To them the Old Testament was given. The church exists now in every land among every people, and to them the completed Scriptures are given. Both are God's chosen people (Deuteronomy 32:9; Ephesians 1:4). Both are redeemed in Jesus Christ (I Corinthians 15:22).

2. *Interpret the Bible literally*. Yes, when that is the way God intended it to be interpreted, but what dispensationalist would interpret the whole Bible literally? "And I saw a beast coming out of the sea. He had ten horns and seven heads . . (Revelation 12:10)." It is not so simple a matter as always trying to find a literal interpretation. We must always seek to understand the Bible as it was intended to be understood. If this is literal then that is how we must understand it. But if figurative speech is used, we must understand it as such.

3. *Salvation is one program God is using to glorify himself, but it is not the only program.* The first question of the Westminster Catechism is: "What is the chief end of man?" The answer is: ". . . . to glorify God, and to enjoy him forever." Man's purpose in the covenantal scheme is to glorify God. No covenantal theologian would claim that God's only plan for glorifying himself is salvation in a narrow sense of that word. But God's whole plan from beginning to end is to glorify himself, and this plan all centers in Jesus Christ who came that men might have access to the Father.

I am the way, and the truth, and the life. No one comes to the Father except through me.

> John 14:6 NIV

For God so loved the world that he gave his one and only Son, that whoever believes in him shall not perish but have eternal life.

> John 3:16 NIV

Conclusion

What is precious to the covenant theologian may be summed up as follows:

Covenant Theology

Whatever comes to pass, comes to pass by the will of God.
1. God is sovereign in salvation.
2. God has a singularity of purpose in dealing with mankind.
3. God's dealing with mankind in this manner is reflected in the biblical covenants.

To the covenant theologian these are more significant factors than the difference in economies God uses in governing the world.

[1] Charles Caldwell Ryrie, *the Ryrie Study Bible* (Chicago: Moody, 1976).

[2] Charles Caldwell Ryrie, *Dispensationalism Today* (Chicago: Moody, 1965).

[3] From *The Twentieth Century Encylopedia of Religious Knowledge* by Schaff and Herzog. Reprinted and used by permission of Baker Book House.

Questions for Review

1. Characterize a dispensationalist position.

2. Characterize a covenantal position.

3. What do covenantal theologians and dispensationalists have in common?

4. How old is dispensationalism? Covenantal theology?

Questions for Discussion

1. Why do you think some dispensationalists are so critical of covenantal theologians and *vice versa*?

2. Does one have to be either a dispensationalist or a covenantal theologian?

3. When the author of the epistle to the Hebrews uses Jeremiah 31:31 in chapter eight of Hebrews, does this give any additional understanding of how the apostles used the Old Testament?

4. Why do you accept or reject the position of covenantal theology?

13

THE LONG WAIT

Biblical Text: Revelation 18–19

In Revelation 18 we read a prophecy about the fall of Babylon. Babylon—known from the Old Testament—had been destroyed many years before. The Babylon spoken about here is a picture of the Roman Empire as the persecutor of Christians.

Revelation 19 contains two visions. First is the vision of a great multitude in heaven praising God. The second vision is of a Rider on a White Horse whose name is the Word of God. This is a picture of the victorious Christ.

The kingdom of heaven is here! The fullness of times is here! So how come we are getting persecuted? Why are there wars? Why does the church have hypocrites in it? The answers to these questions are the substance of the book of Revelation.

The age awaited since creation—the age of man's rule—has begun. God gave man the mandate at creation to subdue the earth and rule over the animals. This ought to be the day of victory for the church. The message of the book of Revelation is a message about the victorious church, but there are a few things that will transpire before the end. The book of Revelation is about these things.

In the message of Jesus there was an emphasis on fulfillment of the Old Testament expectations in his message that the kingdom had come and that Christ was now the way to God. There was also, however, an element of still future expectation in his statements. Jesus said, "I go to prepare a place for you." This statement implies some of the kingdom work is still future. He also spoke about the growth of the kingdom to fullness and about coming judgment. In these statements were the initial indication that while the kingdom had come and Christ fulfilled the law and the prophets there was, nevertheless, a messianic work which would be ongoing.

Paul too has an element in his message which indicates that there is an ongoing aspect to the work of Christ. Paul speaks of the fullness of times, but also of this present evil age, and looks forward to Christ's coming.

The author of the epistle to the Hebrews spoke of the Old Testament as a shadow and said that now we have the heavenly reality through Christ. He also pointed out that God's creation purpose for man to rule was not yet accomplished, except in the person of Jesus Christ who was our pioneer. Such implies that we must eventually follow and that this work is still going on.

Tradition tells us that John was the disciple of Christ who lived the longest. John, more than any other apostle, became aware of the ongoing aspects of Christ's work. He realized, as disciple after disciple passed on, that Christ's coming would probably not be in his lifetime. The proclamation had for many of those early years been: the kingdom has come, the last days are upon us, and the fullness of times is here. As time went on, it became more and more clear that a large part of the Christian's work was dealing with the circumstances of living in the fullness of times but having the present age still very much with us.

For centuries the Jewish hope was for the coming of the Messiah, the coming of the kingdom, the coming of *that day*. Now that it is here and persecutions and suffering are still with us, what hope is there for the Christian's future? What does the Christian have to look forward to besides more of what we already have? John writes late in his life about this matter.

The Significance of the Sevens

Many commentaries on the book of Revelation comment on the fact that the number seven is very prominent in the book. There are

The Roman Empire
In the 1st Century A.D.

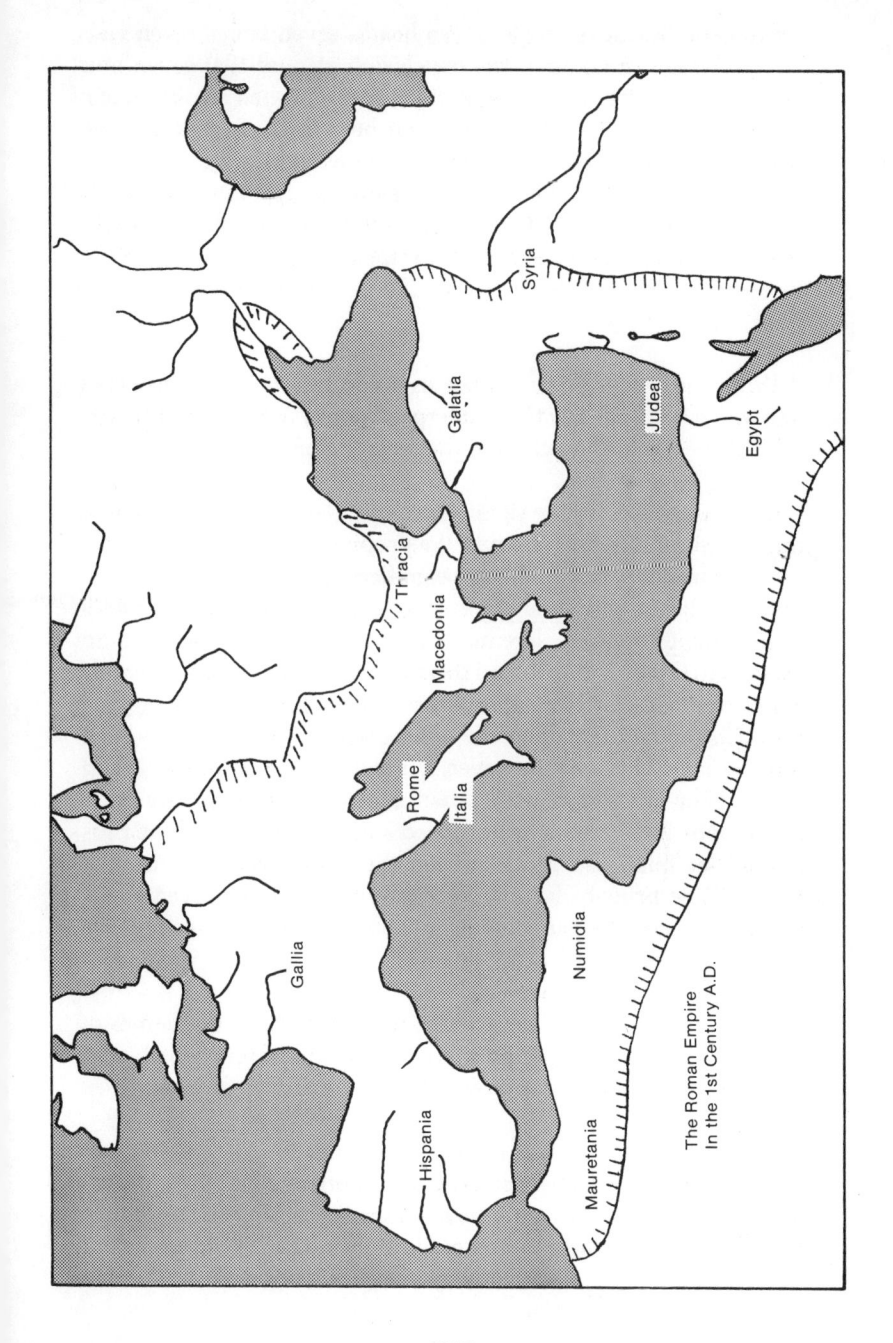

seven churches, seven seals, seven heads, seven kings, seven vials, etc. Anyone can come to the conclusion at once that seven must signify something. Many suggestions regarding the significance of "seven" in the book of Revelation have been made. In seeking to understand the significance of "seven," we would do well to use the principles which we have used previously for interpreting the parables of Jesus (1) Seek to understand the Bible in the way it was intended to be understood (2) Look for the interpretation in the Scriptures themselves (3) Be careful not to see meaning where there is none.

While the first principle is the most important one, it is the second one which holds the key to the interpretation. We must ask: Does the Bible itself give us any clues to the meaning of "seven"?

One suggestion for the significance of the sevens is to be found in the way seven has been used in the prophetic books. Since Revelation is a prophetic book, this is a significant suggestion. The suggestion is to begin with Jeremiah's prophecy of judgment on Israel in chapter 25:8-11. Here Jeremiah says that because Israel has not listened to God, God will send them into exile for 70 years. Here the length of time, seventy years, is a threat. It is a long time. In Jeremiah 29:4-23, the fact that the exile will be seventy years long is mentioned again. This time, however, it is in a letter to the people in captivity. They are told to settle down, and seek the prosperity of the city to which they have been carried so that they too will be prosperous. Jeremiah also says that when the seventy years are finished, they will be brought back from captivity. Here the seventy year period becomes a blessing. It will only be seventy years, and it will be a good seventy years.

In both of these prophecies the period is seventy, and there is no question but what the period marks the length of time which must pass before the next gracious act of God towards his people.

The prophet Daniel was among those in exile. As he grew older these words of Jeremiah must have been upon his mind. In his old age he saw the period of seventy years approaching an end. In chapter nine of Daniel we read a prayer made by Daniel in his old age asking

God to look with favor on his people who are in exile. When he is finished praying, he has a vision—the vision which has become known as the vision of the seventy sevens.

Now a discussion of the vision of the seventy sevens in Daniel could lead us very far afield of our purpose here—to study Revelation. The important thing to note, however, is what this vision says and what the significance of the sevens is. Setting aside all of the various suggestions for the interpretation of this propehcy, we want to limit our investigation to two questions: What is the general message of the prophecy to Israel, and what do the sevens indicate.

First of all it is clear, regardless of what else one may want to say about the prophecy, that the message is: Many things must yet transpire before the Anointed One comes. Or put another way, the message is: Some time will yet transpire before the next great act of God.

Now, the writer of the book of Revelation knew the Old Testament very well. It is likely that he knew it much better then the average Christian today. It is also true that his readers also were familiar with the Old Testament. These facts are reflected in the ways that certain clues to the meaning of Revelation can be found in the Old Testament and were probably obvious to the first readers of the book of Revelation. For example—in Revelation 10:5-7 we read about an angel who raises his hand and swears. This is reminicent of Deuteronomy 32:40 when God lifts his hand to heaven and swears. Here the act is a prelude to judgment, and the readers of Revelation would know the significance of the angel's raised hand because of their familiarity with Deuteronomy 32.

The significance of the various sevens used in Revelation would seem to be that John is telling the early church that time must pass before Christ's coming. When they heard of seven vials, seven seals, and seven kings, they would recall the 70 years of captivity and the seventy sevens of Daniel. They would realize that there would be a long wait for Christ's coming.

The Fall of Babylon
and the Rider on the White Horse

There are numerous things in the book of Revelation which are symbolic such as the sevens, but the content also contains a message. It is not possible to review the whole book of Revelation in this study, but a closer look at a portion of it will help us understand its message and how it fits into the overall message of the New Testament.

Chapters 18 and 19 contain visions which typify the message of Revelation. Chapter 18 is about the fall of Babylon, and chapter 19 is about the triumph of the people of God.

Babylon was the name of the capital city of Nebechadnezzer who had taken the people of Jerusalem into exile in Old Testament times. At the time John wrote the book of Revelation, it had creased to exist as a world power. The Babylon referred to here cannot be the same, but the use of the name Babylon brings to mind the captivity of Israel and its suffering under a pagan nation and king.

The extended announcement in chapter 18 of the fall of Babylon would seem to be a message about the people of God in John's day eventually being delivered from the persecutions under which they were suffering. The identification of "Babylon" with the Roman Empire seems obvious from numerous aspects of the description found in chapter 18, previous references in Revelation to Babylon, and from other New Testament references to Babylon. It is beyond the scope of this study to digress on the identification of Babylon. The important observation is that John says the kingdom persecuting the people of God will itself be overthrown and judged for its persecutons.

Chapter 19 leaves off the description of the fall of Babylon and takes up with the vision of a "great multitude" which is singing praises to God in heaven. In verse 11 the vision turns to the description of a rider on a white horse. The rider is called "Faithful and True." He is dressed in a "robe dipped in blood, and his name is the Word of God." There is no doubt whatsoever that this is a vision of the Messiah in triumph and judgment. In <u>verse 19</u> John reports that the armies of the earth gather to make war against him but they are defeated. The message of John is that there will be a time of rejoicing in heaven when Christ is ultimately victorious over all his enemies. Note too that the rejoicing is that of a "great multitude."

Summary

At <u>creation</u> God gave man the <u>responsibility</u> to subdue the earth and rule over the animals <u>(Genesis 1:28)</u>. The writer of the epistle to the Hebrews taught us that, while we do not yet see all things in subjection to man, Christ has become the first fruits of his people in that he has now been exalted.

God had promised David a son who would have an eternal throne. The apostles in their sermons which are recorded in the book of Acts, tell us that Jesus Christ is this son. Jesus himself told us that the kingdom had come.

John in the book of Revelation does not tell us anything contrary to what we have found in the other books of the New Testament, but he has explained an aspect of it which we did not previously see quite so clearly. (1) The kingdom has come, but here will be many sevens before the final victory of Christ over all the kings and armies of the earth. (2) Eventually Babylon—Rome, and for that matter every kingdom which will persecute the people of God—will be destroyed. (3) There will be a great day of rejoicing in heaven a) by a great multitude of God's people, b) when the Messiah ultimately judges his enemies.

The message of Revelation is a message of caution for days of optimism, that many persecutions lay ahead. It is also a message of hope for dark days, that Christ will ultimately be victorious.

Questions for Review

1. What is the opinion of the author of this book as to the significance of the "sevens" in the book of Revelation?

2. What is the context of Revelation chapters 18 and 19?

3. What three principles should we use to interpret Revelation?

4. What are three things we learn from John in Revelation?

Questions for Discussion

1. Is this interpretation of Revelation different than interpretations you have heard before? In what way is it different?

2. Do you agree with the author's interpretation of the significance of the "sevens"? Why?

3. Does the explanation of the message of Revelation given in this book fit in with a premillennial view? An amillennial view? A postmillennial view?

4. Which view do you think the author takes?

5. In the questions at the end of chapter 1, you were asked: What are your expectations for this course? Has this study met your expectations?

Bibliography

Adams, Jay E. *The Time is at Hand*. Presbyterian and Reformed, 1970.
An amillennialist view of the book of Revelation; 106 pages.

Boettner, Loraine. *The Millennium*. Grand Rapids: Baker, 1958.
A postmillennialist exposition.

Hughes, Philip Edgcumbe. *A Commentary on the Epistle to the Hebews*.
Grand Rapids: Eerdmans, 1977.
An excellent commentary on Hebrews.

Ladd, George Eldon. *The Blessed Hope*. Grand Rapids: Eerdmans, 1956.
A premillennial exposition.

Longenecker, Richard N. *Biblical Exegesis in the Apostolic Period*.
Grand Rapids: Eerdmans, 1975.
A thorough discussion of the apostolic use of the Old Testament.

Ridderbos, Herman. *The Coming of the Kingdom*. Philadelphia:
Presbyterian and Reformed, 1962.
Heavy but very helpful.

_____ . *Paul, An Outline of His Theology*. Grand Rapids: Eerdmans, 1975.
Again, heavy but helpful.

Robertson, O. Palmer. *The Christ of the Covenants*. Grand Rapids:
Baker, 1980.
An excellent overview of God's covenantal dealings with mankind; recommended reading.

Ryrie, Charles Caldwell. *Dispensationalism Today*. Chicago: Moody, 1965.
Perhaps the best defense of the dispensational position.

Vos, Geerhardus. *The Kingdom of God and the Church*. Nutley, N.J.:
Presbyterian and Reformed, 1972.
An excellent discussion of the kingdom concept in the New Testament; 124 pages.

_____ . *The Pauline Eschatology*. Grand Rapids: Eerdmans, 1972.
Difficult for the layman, but very good if one can manage it.

_____ . *The Teaching of the Epistle to the Hebrews*. Nutley, N.J.:
Presbyterian and Reformed, 1977.
A discussion of important aspects of Hebrews; 124 pages.